READING COMPREHENSION
GRADES 2-3

 VOL. 5 Teacher Resources for Blended Learning

Teacher Resources for Blended Learning

Vol. 1
Print Concepts & Phonological Awareness

Vol. 2
Letter Sounds

Vol. 3
Decodable Words, Sight Words & Spelling

Vol. 4
Reading Comprehension: Grades K-1

Vol. 5
Reading Comprehension: Grades 2–3

Vol. 6
Reading Comprehension: Grades 4+

Vol. 7
Grammar, Vocabulary, Speaking & Listening

Available at imaginelearning.com/bookstore

September 2016 Edition

ISBN 978-1-945460-04-3

CONTENTS

READING COMPREHENSION GRADES 2–3

This section includes activities, resources, and lessons to help students build reading fluency and improve comprehension skills.

Reteaching Lessons 259

Identify struggling students with the Action Areas Tool and use these lessons to intervene and reteach reading comprehension skills.

Notes

Using Imagine Learning in the Classroom

Blended Learning with Imagine Learning

Along with the lessons and activities in this volume, Imagine Learning offers a wealth of digital instructional activities. Used together, the offline and online teaching materials provide teachers more flexibility to teach language and literacy within a blended learning environment.

Implementation Options

Offline lessons and online resources can be used for whole group lessons, small group interventions, or individual coaching sessions. Imagine Learning's individualized learning paths also allow students to learn independently at their own individual levels.

TEACHER-LED INSTRUCTION

Because Imagine Learning activities teach key language and literacy skills, teachers can select desired lessons for focused whole-class instruction, practice, and review. Projecting activities or using them with an interactive white board makes it easy for everyone to participate.

ONE-ON-ONE INSTRUCTION

Teachers can use the Action Areas Tool to gain insight on where individual students are struggling and use that information to provide focused instruction. This data is especially helpful as you create an RTI plan and work on skills remediation. Teachers can also extend learning by reviewing student recordings and written responses to offer direct feedback.

SMALL-GROUP INSTRUCTION

The Action Areas Tool pinpoints where groups of students are struggling and immediately creates skill-based intervention groups. The tool also suggests online activities and reteaching lessons that allow for targeted intervention.

COMPUTER BANK OR LAB ROTATION

Imagine Learning provides each student with an individualized learning path by providing systematic, adaptive instruction. This makes it ideal for independent student learning—whether it be at an in-class station or in a computer lab.

Digital Imagine Learning Activities

Teachers can access Imagine Learning's engaging digital activities through the Activity Menu. The Activity Menu is organized by curriculum area. For digital activities that match the skills in this volume, click the corresponding curriculum area. Use the functions below to find the best settings for your class.

Change **program settings,** including first-language support.

Launch the **Imagine Learning Portal** to find reports, management functions, and additional resources.

Enter the **Imagine Museum** to preview performance-based student engagement features.

Log out of the Activity Menu and return to the **login page.**

Reports and Tools

Tools for setting up the program and monitoring student progress and growth are provided to teachers and administrators. Reviewing data regularly, as well as analyzing student recordings and writings, drives program efficacy and success.

Review group and individual student data, and listen to student recordings.

Launch Activity Menu and Teacher Resources.

Manage classroom and student account preferences (session time, student passwords, etc.).

Action Areas Tool

Use data from the Action Areas Tool to identify individual students or groups of students that struggle with a particular skill. Action Areas will also suggest online activities that can be used to help struggling students.

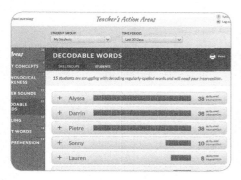 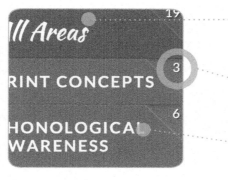

The left navigation pane lists all curriculum areas.

This number denotes how many students are struggling in a curriculum area.

Click a curriculum area and click **Intervention Tools** to view details, suggested activities, and printouts.

Teacher Resources

All Classroom Activities and Reteaching Lessons included in this volume can also be found in the Teacher Resources section online.

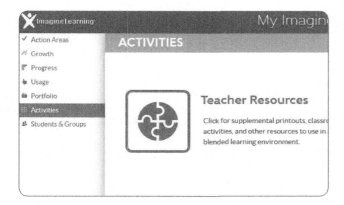 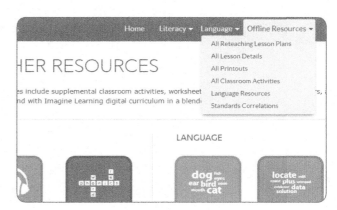

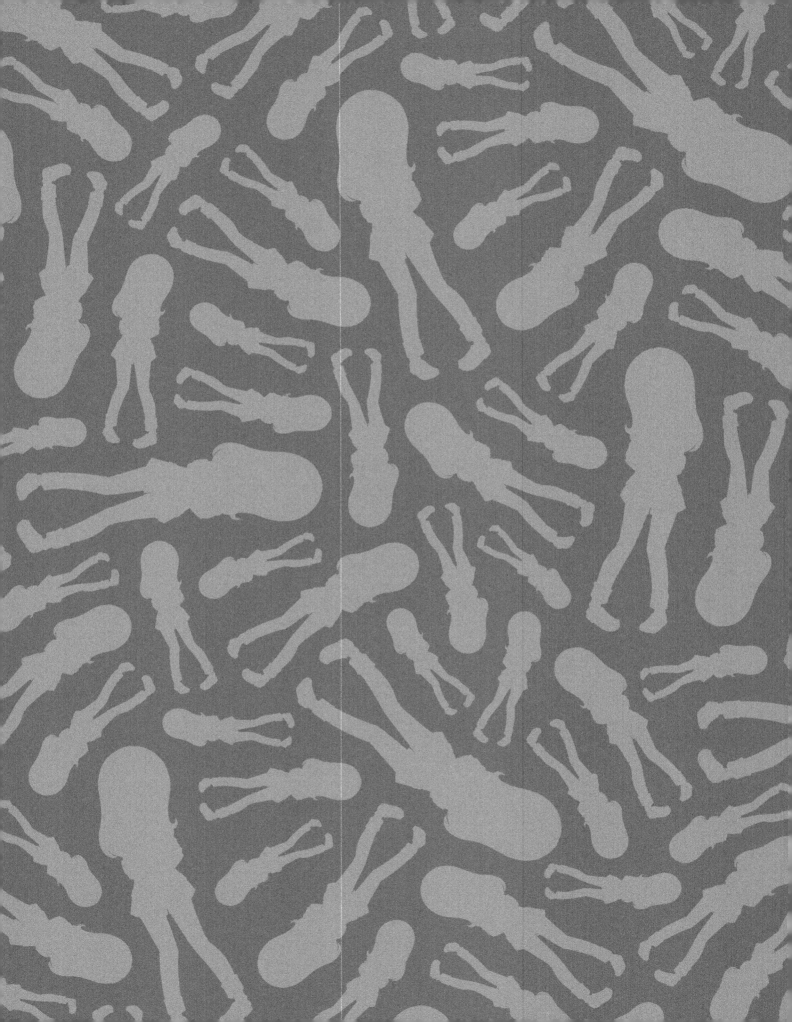

READING COMPREHENSION GRADES 2–3

CLASSROOM ACTIVITIES

Classroom activities include ideas and resources for whole-class or small group work to help students develop literacy and comprehension skills. The print-ready texts provide opportunities to build fluency and reinforce and extend the skills students learn from the Imagine Learning online curriculum.

- A variety of literary and informational texts that fit multiple instructional needs and settings
- Standards-based materials that require minimal teacher preparation
- Leveled reading passages and corresponding printouts such as comprehension questions, graphic organizers, and response journals
- Comprehension strategies to help students understand and critically analyze texts

Fiction or Nonfiction

Classroom Activities

LEARNING OBJECTIVE: Distinguish between fiction and nonfiction books.

LANGUAGE OBJECTIVE: Talk about the differences between fiction and nonfiction texts.

Activity Overview

Students listen to passages, discuss fiction and nonfiction, then complete a sorting activity about the differences between fiction and nonfiction books.

Materials	Preparation
• Sorting Cards (one set per student pair or group) • Story Record printout (optional) • Large poster board (optional)	• Cut out Sorting Cards (or have students cut out their own sorting cards).

Explain

Say: ***Books and stories can be fiction or nonfiction. Fiction stories are created by the author's imagination and are written to entertain the reader. Nonfiction stories are true stories or books created to give the reader information.***

Say: ***I will read two short passages. One is fiction. The other is nonfiction. Listen carefully to tell me which one is which.***

Read the passages to the students. Have children identify which story is fiction, which is nonfiction, and what elements help them to know.

Passage 1: Thumbelina

An old woman went to a fairy and said, "I should so very much like to have a little child. Can you tell me where I can find one?" The fairy gave her a special seed and told her to return home and plant the seed in a flowerpot. She planted it, and immediately a large beautiful flower, like a tulip, bloomed in the pot. The woman kissed the dark green leaves, and as she did, the flower opened. Inside was a very delicate, very tiny maiden, not even three inches tall. She had soft skin like a flower petal and silky, golden hair. The woman named her Thumbelina because she was so small.

Thumbelina had many wild and sometimes frightening adventures with creatures of the woods, including being kidnapped by singing frogs, traveling with butterflies, being teased by cockroaches, and making friends with a swallow.

She flew on the swallow's back to a meadow of flowers where she discovers that in each flower lives a tiny fairy person, just like her. When the prince of the land meets Thumbelina, he offers her his golden crown and asks her if she will be his princess.

Passage 2: The Glory Bush

The Glory Bush is a small flowering tree originally from the tropical rainforest in southern Brazil. It is also known as the Princess Flower. It has beautiful pinkish red buds that open into three-inch-wide purple flowers. Each individual flower doesn't last long, but new blooms open all summer. The deep-green leaves are covered with short, silky hairs that make them feel soft and velvety.

The Princess Flower can reach up to two or three feet tall when planted in a pot. If placed outside, Princess Flowers attract bees, butterflies, and other garden creatures. To care for a Princess Flower, place the plant in full sun. Water the plant regularly to prevent it from drying out. Watch out for spider mites, who like to eat the leaves.

Possible Discussion Elements	
Thumbelina: Fiction	**The Glory Bush: Nonfiction**
Fairies	A flower that comes from a real place (Brazil)
A tiny person the size of a thumb	True facts and information about the flower
Talking and singing animals	Directions or instructions
Riding on a swallow	Things that real animals do
Characters that live in flowers	

Play

1. Divide students into pairs or small groups.

2. Give each pair or group a set of sorting cards.

3. Have students take turns sorting the cards into two piles, one for fiction and one for nonfiction.

EXTENSION ACTIVITY:

For the next month, each time you read a story to the class, have the students decide if the story is fiction or nonfiction and tell why they think so. Record their responses on the Fiction or Nonfiction Story List or create a classroom poster. Fill in the titles of the stories you read and have a student place a sticker in the appropriate Fiction or Nonfiction column next to each story.

Fantasy, not real	True facts
Made-up characters	Real people
Imaginary setting	Maps, charts, and graphs
Tells an entertaining story	Directions or instructions
Read just for enjoyment	Read for enjoyment and to learn
Funny or silly pictures	Photos or realistic drawings
Must read from beginning to end	Can be read in any order
Entertains us	Gives us information
Wild and crazy adventures	Real events
Talking things or animals	Real things and animals

Book Title	Fiction	Nonfiction

Story Record

Transition Books Guide

About Transition Books

Transition Books are informational and literary texts that bridge the gap between decodable texts and leveled texts. The transitions books are thematically arranged and increase in text complexity. Each themed collection includes an informational book and one or two thematically related folktales from different countries. The Transition Book printouts that support reading and vocabulary are:

- Transition Book Texts and Comprehension Questions
- Word Cards

Transition Book Texts and Comprehension Questions

Resource Overview

Transition Books texts are blackline masters of the informational book texts and folktale texts. Each Transition Book text also includes an Oral Reading Fluency assessment box to evaluate students' oral reading ability. Transition Books include words with advanced letter sounds, multisyllabic words, and compound words. Refer to the Transition Books Reference Chart to see the words targeted in each book.

The Comprehension Questions printouts have students answer literal and inferential questions about events in the story as well as questions about the story lesson in the fables and folktales. Answers to questions are located in the Transition Books Answer Key.

How to Use This Resource in the Classroom

Informational Texts

- Before reading, preview the text to identify words that students might find difficult to pronounce and words that might have unfamiliar meanings. Review the words with students and explain their meanings. Point out the words and their meanings while reading the book.
- While students follow along, read the text aloud at a pace that is slightly slower than normal. Encourage students to track words with a finger if they need to.
- After reading, ask students to connect the story to another text they have read.
- Have partners take turns reading sections or paragraphs, or have them read aloud simultaneously.
- Have partners discuss their favorite part or share interesting new facts they learned from the text.

Fables and Folktales

- Read all but the last few pages of the story and have children guess what the lesson of the story is.
- Show or read the title of the story. State the story lesson before you read the story. Have the students discuss the meaning and guess how the lesson might be taught or who might need to learn the lesson.
- Have the group act out the fable. Form a circle. The center of the circle is a stage. Choose a narrator and actors for each part. The narrator tells the story in his or her own words and the actors add in lines and perform the action. The remaining students in the circle are the audience.
- Explain to students that any book can be told as an oral story. Storytellers take existing stories and use their imaginations, body movements, and expressive tones of voice to retell the story in their own way. Using quotes from the book or lines they write themselves, have students write a script for a scene from the story. Have students add notes that describe how the characters should move or act as they speak.
- Have students work individually or in small groups to use the folktale model to create an original folktale or rewrite a fable in a modern setting.

✗ Imagine Learning®

Word Cards

Resource Overview

The Transition Book Word Cards contain multisyllable and compound words from each book. This resource helps students learn to decode multisyllabic words by breaking words apart and applying common letter-sound correspondences and recognizing common syllabication patterns.

How to Use This Resource in the Classroom

Multisyllable Words

- Use the multisyllable Word Cards and have students repeat the word after you. Have students say the word again and clap or tap the number of syllables. Have students again clap each syllable and say the word, but this time leave out the first syllable in the word (for example, say "delicious" without the *de*: "-licious.") Repeat again and delete the ending or middle syllable.

- Review with students that words can be separated into syllables and that each syllable contains a vowel. Explain to the students that they can move syllables around to make a new silly word that has no meaning. Use the multisyllable Word Cards. Have students identify the syllables in that word and then move one of the syllables to a different position in the word (for example: pencil = cilpen, backpack = packback, computer = tercompu).

- Divide the multisyllable words from the Word Cards into syllables and write each syllable on an index card. Display the syllables in jumbled order and have students arrange the syllables to form the words.

Compound Words

- Give index cards to the students. Have them use the compound words on the Word Cards and copy each half of the word onto a separate index card (for example: *air, plane, humming, bird*). Shuffle index cards together and pass out one card to each student. Instruct the students to find the word that will match with their word to create the original compound word. Have students move around the room to find their match. Once a match has been made, have the pair stand together until you check to make sure their word is correct.

- Have students choose a compound word from the Word Cards to make a shutter-flap foldable. Use a plain sheet of white paper in (landscape position). Fold the ends of the paper in to make shutters. The students will break apart the compound word and write one part on each flap. Underneath the flaps, students will rewrite the compound word together. They can also write the definition and draw a picture to go along with the compound word.

Transition Books Reference Chart

Theme	Book Title	Story Lesson	Compound Words	Multisyllable Words
Am I Too Small?	What Happened to Pluto		—	planet, farthest, system, smallest, solar, scientist
	The Lion and the Mouse *a fable from Greece*	Even something small can be a great help.	something	finally, gnawing, suddenly, focused, grateful
Let's Fly	First Flight		daytime	brothers, blowing, engine, slower, lifted
	The Hummingbird and the Crane *a Native American folktale*	Slow and steady wins the race.	nearby, hummingbird	continued, replied, steady, already
To the Races	A Tugboat Race on the Hudson		tugboats	narrow, waiting, captains, river, fancy
	The Tiger and the Fox *a fable from Japan*	Don't tease others.	—	stronger, shoulder, mountains, believe, behind, notice
Strong Winds	Tornadoes		outside	brewing, tornado, funnels, powerful, minutes
	The Sun and the North Wind *a fable from Greece*	You can be both gentle and powerful.	whoever, himself	calmly, gently, neither, giant
What's to Eat?	Making Sushi		seaweed, crabmeat, chopsticks	sushi, tightly, enjoy
	Stone Soup *a folktale from France*	You can do great things when you share and work together.	everyone, goodbye	delicious, together, stirring, moment
	The Story of Watermelon *a folktale from Vietnam*	Problems can be overcome by working hard.	watermelon, overcome, everything	symbol, island, juicy
Finding a Fortune	Gold		without	California, thousands, harder, miners, started
	King Midas *a story from Greece*	Some things are more important than gold.	rainbow	surprised, daughter, beautiful, furniture, important
	The Fisherman and His Wife *a folktale from Germany*	Don't be greedy.	fisherman	realized, angry, golden, mansion, cottage

Transition Books Reference Chart
Copyright © Imagine Learning, Inc.

Transition Books Answer Key

Book Title	Q1	Q2	Q3	Q4
What Happened to Pluto	a	c	b	a
The Lion and the Mouse	d	b	a	b
First Flight	c	b	a	c
The Hummingbird and the Crane	d	a	b	c
A Tugboat Race on the Hudson	b	a	c	d
The Tiger and the Fox	b	a	a	c
Tornadoes	b	a	c	a
The Sun and the North Wind	d	c	c	a
Making Sushi	b	a	c	d
Stone Soup	b	b	a	a
The Story of Watermelon	c	a	d	a
Gold	b	c	a	a
King Midas	d	a	a	c
The Fisherman and His Wife	a	d	a	c

Classroom Activities

Name: _____

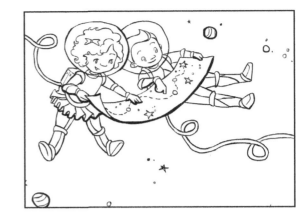

What Happened to Pluto?

Written by Nari Carter
Illustrated by Hollie Hibbert
Lexile®: 440L, 96 words

Earth is a planet. Mars is a planet.

Pluto **was** a planet. Now it is not.

Pluto was the farthest and smallest planet in our solar system.

Then, scientists said it wasn't a planet. So, what's up with that?

It's not that Pluto dropped out of space. Pluto is still out there.

Scientists just changed their ideas about what a planet is. Now, Pluto is called a dwarf planet.

Dwarf planets are too small to be planets.

Scientists believe there are other dwarf planets in our solar system.

Maybe you will find the next dwarf planet.

Accuracy: # of reading errors: _____ (Indep. = 0–2, Instr. = 3–5, Frust. = 6+)	
Speed: To calculate: 5760 ÷ _____ (Reading time in seconds) = _____ WPM	

Imagine Learning®

Name

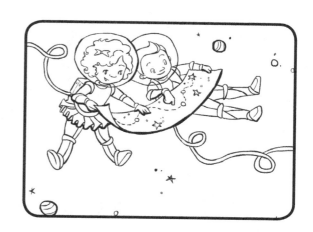

What Happened to Pluto?
Comprehension Questions

1. **What is Pluto called now?**
   a. a dwarf planet
   b. a solar system
   c. a space dwarf
   d. a solar dwarf

2. **Dwarf Planets are _____ than other planets.**
   a. bigger
   b. hotter
   c. smaller
   d. colder

3. **What do we learn about scientists from this passage?**
   a. They go into space.
   b. They change their ideas.
   c. They think there is only one dwarf planet.
   d. They think Pluto is a planet.

4. **What is the main idea of this passage?**
   a. Pluto is too small to be a planet.
   b. Pluto is far away.
   c. Dwarf planets drop out of space every year.
   d. All dwarf planets are called Pluto.

 **Imagine Learning®**

Comprehension Questions: What Happened to Pluto

 **WORD CARDS** Cut out the cards and practice learning the words.

planet	farthest
system	smallest
solar	scientists

Word Cards: What Happened to Pluto
Copyright © Imagine Learning, Inc.

Name: _____

The Lion and the Mouse

Adapted by Amy Morris
Illustrated by Brian Taylor
Lexile®: 450L, 180 words

Lion was sleeping in the warm sun. Suddenly he felt something run across his face.

Lion opened his eyes and swiftly caught a tiny mouse. Lion was hungry and about to eat Mouse when he heard her little voice.

"Please don't eat me! If you let me go, one day I will help you!" Mouse said.

Lion laughed. "What can a little thing like you do for me? You are so small, you could never help me."

But Lion was in a good mood. He let Mouse go.

Later that day, Lion was hunting. He was so focused on his prey that he didn't see a net.

Lion got caught in the net. He roared and clawed at the ropes, but he could not get free.

Mouse heard Lion's mighty roar and ran to help. Mouse began gnawing the rope with her teeth.

Mouse chewed through the rope and set Lion free. Lion was amazed and grateful.

"Even though you are small, you saved me!" said Lion.

"Finally you see!" said Mouse. "Even something small can be a great help!"

Accuracy: # of reading errors: _____ (Indep. = 0–4, Instr. = 5–9, Frust. = 10+)
Speed: To calculate: 10800 ÷ _____ (Reading time in seconds) = _____ WPM

Name

The Lion and the Mouse
Comprehension Questions

1. **What mistake did Mouse make at the beginning of the story?**

   a. She got caught in a net.

   b. She ran away from Lion.

   c. She fell asleep near Lion.

   d. She ran across Lion's face.

2. **Why did Lion think Mouse couldn't help him?**

   a. She was too silly.

   b. She was too small.

   c. She was very rude.

   d. She was very hungry.

3. **What did Mouse do to help Lion?**

   a. She chewed through the net.

   b. She woke him up from a nap.

   c. She listened to him roar.

   d. She crawled across his nose.

4. **What lesson did Lion learn?**

   a. Small things are not helpful.

   b. Even something small can be of great help.

   c. It's important to be focused on hunting.

   d. Claws can be used to get out of a net.

Comprehension Questions: The Lion and the Mouse
Copyright © Imagine Learning, Inc.

Cut out the cards and practice learning the words.

something	finally
gnawing	suddenly
focused	grateful

Name: _____

First Flight

Written by Nari Carter
Illustrated by Jim Madsen
Lexile®: 390L, 96 words

Classroom Activities

It was daytime. They were on a beach. The winds were blowing at 20 miles per hour.

The Wright brothers looked at each other. Should they still do what they had planned? Yes.

Orville turned on the engine, and Wilbur unhooked the rope. Then the plane moved.

At 10:35 in the morning, it lifted into the air for the first time. Hooray!

The plane flew over 120 feet. It didn't go fast. Its top speed was only 6.8 miles per hour. That's slower than a bike.

But the plane went up, and air flight was real!

Accuracy: # of reading errors: _____ (Indep. = 0–2, Instr. = 3–5, Frust. = 6+)
Speed: To calculate: 5760 ÷ _____ (Reading time in seconds) = _____ WPM

Transition Books: First Flight
Copyright © Imagine Learning, Inc.

ImagineLearning®

Name

First Flight
Comprehension Questions

1. **Where did the first flight take place?**
   a. at an airport
   b. in a bike shop
   c. at a beach
   d. in the desert

2. **What did Wilbur have to do before the plane moved?**
   a. run as fast as he could
   b. unhook the rope
   c. pedal the bike
   d. wait for a strong wind

3. **How fast did the plane fly?**
   a. 6.8 miles per hour
   b. 120 miles per hour
   c. 20 miles per hour
   d. 10.35 miles per hour

4. **How did the brothers feel about the flight?**
   a. mad
   b. afraid
   c. happy
   d. sad

WORD CARDS Cut out the cards and practice learning the words.

daytime	brothers
blowing	engine
slower	lifted

Word Cards: First Flight
Copyright © Imagine Learning, Inc.

Imagine Learning®

Name: _____

The Hummingbird and the Crane

Adapted by Danny Eggers
Illustrated by Jim Madsen
Lexile®: 430L, 251 words

Once there were two birds. Hummingbird was small and quick. She was proud of her speed.

Crane was large and slow. Hummingbird often made fun of Crane.

One day Crane said to Hummingbird, "Let's race to the old tree by the river. The first one to the top of the tree wins." Crane knew the tree was very far away.

Hummingbird agreed. She was faster than Crane and knew she could win.

The race began. Hummingbird zipped ahead. She teased Crane for being slow.

Hummingbird saw a flower garden. "I am so far ahead, I can take a break," she thought. Soon she was sipping nectar from the flowers. She forgot all about the race.

Crane flew at a slow and steady pace. She soon passed Hummingbird.

Hummingbird looked up and saw Crane far ahead. "Oh no!" Hummingbird thought as she hurried to catch up.

Hummingbird flew with all her might until she was far ahead of Crane. But Hummingbird saw another garden and again forgot the race.

This continued all day. While Hummingbird zipped from garden to garden, Crane flew at a slow and steady pace.

At sunset, Hummingbird was very far ahead. She decided to rest in a nearby tree. Crane never stopped. She just kept flying.

Hummingbird woke up and hurried to finish the race. When she arrived at the river, Crane was already at the top of the old tree!

"How did you win?" Hummingbird asked. Crane replied, "Don't you know? Slow and steady wins the race."

| Accuracy: # of reading errors: _____ (Indep. = 0–5, Instr. = 6–13, Frust. = 14+) |
| Speed: To calculate: 15060 ÷ _____ (Reading time in seconds) = _____ WPM |

The Hummingbird and the Crane

Comprehension Questions

1. **What was Hummingbird proud of?**
   a. her wings
   b. her beauty
   c. her feet
   d. her speed

2. **Why did Hummingbird lose the race?**
   a. She kept stopping.
   b. She couldn't find the old tree.
   c. She teased Crane.
   d. She got lost in the garden.

3. **Crane flew at a slow and *steady* pace. What does steady mean in the story?**
   a. The tree was firm in the ground.
   b. Crane never stopped flying.
   c. Hummingbird went from garden to garden.
   d. The garden was full of flowers.

4. **What lesson did Hummingbird learn?**
   a. Being small and fast is best.
   b. Being big and slow loses the race.
   c. Slow and steady wins the race.
   d. Flying from garden to garden is best.

Name

Cut out the cards and practice learning the words.

nearby	hummingbird
continued	replied
steady	already

Name: _____

A Tugboat Race on the Hudson

Written by Nari Carter
Illustrated by Hollie Hibbert
Lexile®: 300L, 105 words

The people look at the boats.

These boats aren't fancy or fast. They are tugboats. Their job is to push or pull big ships along the narrow river.

The tugboats can also break up the ice on the river.

But today, they are waiting to race.

The tugboat captains are excited. Each hopes his boat will win.

At noon, the horn sounds. The people cheer.

The tugboats race up the Hudson River.

Soon the boat named Ross Sea is leading. It wins first place with a time of 4:44. All of the other boats were slower.

The captain is proud. His boat is the best!

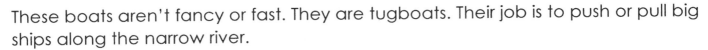

Accuracy: # of reading errors: _____ (Indep. = 0–2, Instr. = 3–6, Frust. = 7+)
Speed: To calculate: 6300 ÷ _____ (Reading time in seconds) = _____ WPM

Name

A Tugboat Race on the Hudson

Comprehension Questions

1. **What are the tugboats waiting to do?**
   a. pull big ships
   b. race each other
   c. break up the ice
   d. take people on a ride

2. **Where does the race take place?**
   a. on a river
   b. on the ocean
   c. on a lake
   d. on the sea

3. **Why was the captain of the Ross Sea proud?**
   a. His boat broke up the most ice.
   b. His boat could push ships through narrow spaces.
   c. His boat was the fastest on the Hudson.
   d. His boat could pull the biggest ships.

4. **Why do the people cheer?**
   a. They want to ride on a tugboat.
   b. They are waiting for their turn to race.
   c. They think the boats are fancy.
   d. They are excited to see the boats race.

Cut out the cards and practice learning the words.

tugboats	narrow
waiting	captains
river	fancy

Word Cards: A Tugboat Race on the Hudson
Copyright © Imagine Learning, Inc.

Name: _____

The Tiger and the Fox

Adapted by Melissa Hart
Illustrated by Hollie Hibbert
Lexile®: 460L, 229 words

Tiger had a problem. He liked to tease his friend Fox.

Every day Tiger would say to Fox, "You're so weak and slow. I am much stronger and faster than you."

One day Tiger had an idea. "Let's race around the world. Then you'll see how fast I am!"

Fox said, "Ok! But if I win you can never tease me again." Fox knew he wasn't as fast as Tiger. But Fox was clever.

Tiger wasn't worried. He knew he would win. Then Tiger could tease Fox even more.

"Ok!" Tiger agreed, grinning. "Ready, set, go!" Tiger yelled as he leaped away, leaving Fox behind.

Tiger was so focused on winning the race that he didn't notice Fox had grabbed his tail. Fox was holding on for the ride.

Tiger ran over mountains, deserts, and plains. He shouted, "I can't even hear you running, Fox. You must be really far behind."

Tiger leaped across lakes and rivers. "You're never going to catch up," Tiger yelled over his shoulder.

Just before the finish line, Tiger stopped to tease Fox again. Fox let go of Tiger's tail and ran. Before Tiger could move, Fox crossed the finish line.

Tiger couldn't believe Fox had won. "I am much faster than you. I should have won."

Fox grinned and said, "If you hadn't stopped to tease me, you would have won the race."

Accuracy: # of reading errors: _____ (Indep. = 0–5, Instr. = 6–12, Frust. = 13+)
Speed: To calculate: 13740 ÷ _____ (Reading time in seconds) = _____ WPM

Name

The Tiger and the Fox
Comprehension Questions

1. **What was Tiger's idea?**
   a. to have Fox hold his tail
   b. to race around the world
   c. to hold Fox's tail
   d. to stop teasing Fox

2. **Why did Fox agree to race?**
   a. so Tiger would stop teasing him
   b. so he could tease Tiger
   c. so he could hold on to Tiger's tail
   d. so he could show how fast he was

3. **How did Fox win?**
   a. He held on to Tiger's tail.
   b. He let Tiger hold his tail.
   c. He ran faster than Tiger.
   d. He jumped over a river.

4. **What lesson did Tiger learn?**
   a. The fastest always wins.
   b. Don't race with a friend.
   c. Don't tease others.
   d. Do anything to win.

 WORD CARDS   Cut out the cards and practice learning the words.

stronger	shoulder
mountains	believe
behind	notice

Name: _____

Tornadoes

Written by Nari Carter
Illustrated by Jim Madsen
Lexile®: 330L, 139 words

The air outside is warm and moist. There are only a few clouds in the sky. It is a hot day.

Later in the day, cool air moves over the land. Wind speed picks up as the cool air meets the warm air.

Dark clouds fill the sky. The winds begin to swirl. A storm is brewing.

Then, a siren blows. It is a warning. A tornado might form.

Tornadoes form during spring and summer. They form when dry, cold air meets warm, moist air.

Tornadoes start in clouds. They are narrow funnels of wind.

Some tornadoes are large and powerful. They can tear trees out of the ground.

Many tornadoes are small. You may not even see them.

But, if you hear a siren, take cover. You only have a few minutes to get to a safe place.

Accuracy: # of reading errors: _____ (Indep. = 0–3, Instr. = 4–7, Frust. = 8+)
Speed: To calculate: 8340 ÷ _____ (Reading time in seconds) = _____ WPM

Transition Books: Tornadoes
Copyright © Imagine Learning, Inc.

Imagine Learning®

Name

Tornadoes
Comprehension Questions

1. **Where do tornadoes begin?**
   a. in trees
   b. in clouds
   c. in covered places
   d. in a safe place

2. **A tornado forms when warm moist air meets _____.**
   a. cold, dry air
   b. dark clouds
   c. narrow wind tunnels
   d. cold, moist air

3. **What should you do if you hear a tornado siren?**
   a. stay outside
   b. stand by a tree
   c. take cover
   d. look for the tornado

4. **Why should you hurry to a safe place if you hear a siren?**
   a. Tornadoes form quickly
   b. Tornadoes can hide
   c. Tornadoes form in clouds
   d. Tornadoes are large and slow

Cut out the cards and practice learning the words.

outside	brewing
tornado	funnels
powerful	minutes

Name: _____

The Sun and the North Wind

Adapted by Holley Mayville
Illustrated by Erin Taylor
Lexile®: 390L, 240 words

Classroom Activities ❖

"I blow roofs off houses and throw giant trees to the ground. I am far more powerful than you," said the North Wind to the Sun.

The Sun replied, "You don't have to be rough to be powerful."

"What do you know?" howled the North Wind. "I'll show you power!" He puffed his cheeks.

"I have an idea. Let's play a game," the Sun said calmly. She pointed to a man walking along an empty road. "Whoever gets his coat off is the most powerful."

"This will be easy," the North Wind laughed. "I'll go first." He took a deep breath and blew as hard as he could at the man below.

The man shivered against the wind. He pulled his coat around himself and walked on.

The North Wind blew again and again. The man wrapped his coat even tighter around himself.

The North Wind was out of breath. He said to the Sun, "I give up. But if I can't do it, neither can you!"

The Sun beamed. "I'll see what I can do." She gently directed her warm glow down on the man. The man began to let go of his coat.

The Sun kept shining her soft rays. Soon the man wiped sweat from his forehead. Then he took off his coat.

The Sun smiled sweetly at the North Wind. "Oh, look," she said, "I did it! It looks like you can be gentle and powerful."

Accuracy: # of reading errors: _____ (Indep. = 0–5, Instr. = 6–12, Frust. = 13+)
Speed: To calculate: 14400 ÷ _____ (Reading time in seconds) = _____ WPM

The Sun and the North Wind
Comprehension Questions

1. **What is one way the North Wind showed he was powerful?**
    a. He played a game.
    b. He held his breath.
    c. He directed his warm glow.
    d. He blew roofs off houses.

2. **What did the man do when the North Wind blew?**
    a. wiped sweat from his forehead
    b. took his coat off
    c. pulled his coat tightly around himself
    d. ran down the empty road

3. **Why did the man take his coat off?**
    a. The North Wind blew very hard.
    b. The North Wind blew roofs off houses.
    c. The Sun warmed him up.
    d. He was at the end of the road.

4. **What lesson did the North Wind learn?**
    a. You can be both gentle and powerful.
    b. Being rough is the most powerful.
    c. Playing games is fun.
    d. Blowing a man's coat off is easy.

Name

 **WORD CARDS**

Cut out the cards and practice learning the words.

whoever	**himself**
calmly	**gently**
neither	**giant**

Word Cards: The Sun and the North Wind

Name: _____

Making Sushi

Written by Sherry Carr
Illustrated by Jim Madsen
Lexile®: 440L, 80 words

Making sushi is easy! First, cook some rice.

When it is done, put it on a plate to cool.

Then lay a long bamboo mat on the table.

Put a sheet of seaweed down on the mat. Brush the seaweed with oil.

Cover the seaweed with rice.

Add fish, crabmeat, peppers, or anything you like.

Roll it up. Then, press it tightly.

Now, cut the roll into many small bites.

It's ready to eat, so grab some chopsticks and enjoy!

Accuracy: # of reading errors: _____ (Indep. = 0–2, Instr. = 3–5, Frust. = 6+)
Speed: To calculate: 4800 ÷ _____ (Reading time in seconds) = _____ WPM

Name

Making Sushi
Comprehension Questions

1. **What is the first step for making sushi?**
   a. roll up the sushi
   b. cook the rice
   c. brush the seaweed with oil
   d. cut the peppers and crabmeat

2. **What do you put on the bamboo mat first?**
   a. seaweed
   b. crabmeat
   c. peppers
   d. rice

3. **To make fresh sushi, it would be good to live _____.**
   a. in the desert
   b. on a mountain
   c. near the sea
   d. on a farm

4. **The author of the story is trying to teach you _____.**
   a. how to use chopsticks
   b. how to make a bamboo mat
   c. how to cook rice
   d. how to make sushi

 Imagine Learning®

 Cut out the cards and practice learning the words.

seaweed	crabmeat
chopsticks	sushi
tightly	enjoy

Word Cards: Making Sushi
Copyright © Imagine Learning, Inc.

Imagine Learning®

Name: _____

Stone Soup

Adapted by Ashley Masters
Illustrated by Erin Taylor
Lexile®: 410L, 269 words

There once was a town with a problem. The people didn't help each other, and they didn't share.

One day a hungry traveler came to town. He asked the people to share their food with him. Everyone said no.

"That's okay," the traveler said. "I will cook stone soup for all of us."

The traveler filled a big pot with water. He took stones from his bag and put them in the pot. He stirred the soup.

People came to see what he was doing. "Stone soup is delicious. But it would be better with onions," the traveler said.

A man thought for a moment. "I can share a few onions," he said. He got some onions and put them in the soup.

The traveler kept stirring and said, "Stone soup is much better with potatoes."

"I can share potatoes," said a woman. She came back with a sack of potatoes for the soup.

"This stone soup would taste great with carrots," said the traveler.

"I'll get carrots!" a boy shouted. He ran home and brought back an armful of carrots to share.

More and more people brought food for the soup. A wonderful smell filled the town. Soon the soup was ready to eat.

Everyone ate until they were full. The soup was delicious! "Look what you did by working together," said the traveler.

The traveler took the stones and put them back in his bag. He waved goodbye. The people were sad to see him leave.

The town was never the same. The people learned that they could do great things when they shared and worked together.

| Accuracy: # of reading errors: _____ (Indep. = 0–6, Instr. = 7–14, Frust. = 15+) |
| Speed: To calculate: 16140 ÷ _____ (Reading time in seconds) = _____ WPM |

Name

Stone Soup
Comprehension Questions

1. **What was one problem the townspeople had?**
    a. They ate too much.
    b. They didn't help each other.
    c. They didn't have vegetables.
    d. They were hungry.

2. **What did the traveler ask the people for?**
    a. a place to rest
    b. to share their food
    c. a bowl of stone soup
    d. work in the town

3. **Why did the people add food to the soup?**
    a. to make the soup taste better
    b. to keep from sharing
    c. to make the town smell good
    d. to keep the food from going bad

4. **What lesson did the people of the town learn?**
    a. how to share and work together
    b. how to ignore travelers
    c. how to grow potatoes
    d. how to keep their food safe

Name

Cut out the cards and practice learning the words.

everyone	goodbye
delicious	together
stirring	moment

Word Cards: Stone Soup
Copyright © Imagine Learning, Inc.

Name: _____

The Story of Watermelon

Adapted by Phung Le
Illustrated by Brian Taylor
Lexile®: 440L, 238 words

Once there was a prince named An-Tiem. He believed that hard work was better than wealth.

"I don't need your money," An-Tiem said to his father, the king. "If I work hard I can get everything I need."

This upset the king. He sent An-Tiem to a distant island without food or tools. The king wanted to teach An-Tiem a lesson.

An-Tiem had to make his own shelter and find his own food. He had to work hard and was often hungry and thirsty.

One day An-Tiem found a large, round fruit. The outside was hard and green. The inside was soft and red with tiny black seeds. It was juicy and delicious.

An-Tiem named the fruit watermelon. "I'll work hard and grow more watermelon!" he said. He dug up the land and planted the seeds.

Soon the island was covered with the fruit. An-Tiem carved a map to the island on a watermelon. He threw it into the sea.

Sailors found the watermelon and came to the island. An-Tiem sailed home on their ship.

An-Tiem took a watermelon to give to his father. The king was happy to see him. An-Tiem told the king all he had done.

An-Tiem showed everyone he could overcome problems by working hard. The king saw that An-Tiem was right.

An-Tiem was made the new king. Watermelon became a symbol of luck. Today people offer it as a present for New Year's.

Accuracy: # of reading errors: _____	(Indep. = 0-5, Instr. = 6–12, Frust. = 13+)
Speed: To calculate: 14280 ÷ _____	(Reading time in seconds) = _____ WPM

Transition Books: The Story of Watermelon
Copyright © Imagine Learning, Inc.

 ImagineLearning®

Name

The Story of Watermelon
Comprehension Questions

1. **What made An-Tiem's father mad?**
   a. An-Tiem went to a distant island to grow watermelon.
   b. An-Tiem was made the new king.
   c. An-Tiem said he could work for what he needed.
   d. An-Tiem ran away to be a sailor.

2. **What did An-Tiem do when he first got to the island?**
   a. built shelter and found food
   b. planted watermelon
   c. carved a map and threw it in the sea
   d. made watermelon a symbol of good luck

3. **Why is watermelon a symbol of luck?**
   a. It is juicy and delicious.
   b. It has a lot of seeds.
   c. It helped An-Tiem get to the island.
   d. It helped An-Tiem return home.

4. **What lesson did the king learn from An-Tiem?**
   a. Problems can be overcome by working hard.
   b. How to carve maps on watermelon.
   c. How to build a shelter and find food.
   d. Planting and growing watermelon is easy.

Name

 **WORD CARDS** Cut out the cards and practice learning the words.

watermelon	overcome
everything	symbol
island	juicy

Word Cards: The Story of Watermelon
Copyright © Imagine Learning, Inc.

 Imagine Learning®

Name: _____

Gold!

Written by Nari Carter
Illustrated by Jim Madsen
Lexile®: 340L, 131 words

Gold! Gold was found in California!

The news spread around the world. Many people left their homes and started for California. They wanted to get rich.

They went by wagon and by boat to get to California. Some even used their feet and walked.

Many miners reached California in 1849. People called them forty-niners.

At first, it was easy to find gold. Gold was on the ground.

Miners just picked it up. Some made thousands of dollars a day.

After a while, it was harder to find gold on the ground.

Forty-niners sifted dirt. They looked in rivers. They even dug up small hills looking for gold.

A few miners got rich. But, most did not find gold.

When the miners went home without gold, they had to start over again.

Accuracy: # of reading errors: _____ (Indep. = 0–3, Instr. = 4–7, Frust. = 8+)
Speed: To calculate: 7860 ÷ _____ (Reading time in seconds) = _____ WPM

Name

Gold!

Comprehension Questions

1. **What is one way miners traveled to California?**

   a. They drove cars.

   b. They walked.

   c. They came on trains.

   d. They came on buses.

2. **What did people call the miners who searched for gold?**

   a. gold diggers

   b. Californians

   c. forty-niners

   d. thousand-dollar men

3. **Where did miners first find gold?**

   a. on the ground

   b. inside hills

   c. in the river

   d. in wagons

4. **What happen to most miners?**

   a. They did **not** get rich.

   b. They found a lot of gold.

   c. They stayed in California.

   d. They did **not** work at banks.

Comprehension Questions: Gold!

Name

 Cut out the cards and practice learning the words.

without	California
thousands	harder
miners	started

Name: _____

King Midas

Adapted by Dianne de Mik
Illustrated by Adam Munoa
Lexile®: 410L, 277 words

King Midas ruled a happy kingdom. He loved his people. He loved his family.

But what he loved the most was his gold. Even though he had piles of gold, he always wanted more.

One day King Midas was in his garden. The flowers were a rainbow of color. Midas didn't see their beauty. "I wish all the flowers were gold!" he thought.

King Midas saw an old man dressed in rags outside the garden. Midas felt sorry for him. He told his servants to give the man food and a place to sleep.

The next morning the old man wanted to thank King Midas. "I will grant you one wish," the old man said.

Without thinking, Midas said, "I wish everything I touch would turn to gold!" The old man bowed and went on his way.

Midas sat down for breakfast. He picked up his fork. It felt heavy in his hand. It had turned to gold! Midas was surprised and grabbed the table. It turned to gold!

Midas ran around the castle touching everything. He turned walls, furniture, and flowers into gold. He was so happy.

At lunchtime his sandwich turned to gold. Midas started to worry. He loved gold, but he was very hungry.

His daughter came into the room. She ran to give Midas a hug. When they touched, she turned into a solid gold statue!

"Oh no! What have I done?" Midas thought. "I should have been more careful with my wish." He ran to find the old man.

"Please take back the wish. I want my daughter back," Midas said. The old man bowed to Midas, and everything returned to normal.

Midas realized that some things are more important than gold.

Accuracy: # of reading errors: _____ (Indep. = 0–6, Instr. = 7–14, Frust. = 15+)
Speed: To calculate: 16620 ÷ _____ (Reading time in seconds) = _____ WPM

Name

King Midas
Comprehension Questions

1. **What did Midas love the most?**
   a. his family
   b. his people
   c. his kingdom
   d. his gold

2. **Why was King Midas given a wish?**
   a. He helped the old man.
   b. He turned the flowers into gold.
   c. He loved his daughter.
   d. He was loved by his kingdom.

3. **What problem did King Midas have after he made his wish?**
   a. He didn't see the beauty in the flowers.
   b. He touched things and they turned to gold.
   c. He couldn't find the old man to thank him.
   d. He had too much food to eat.

4. **What lesson does this story teach?**
   a. There is never enough gold.
   b. All wishes are good.
   c. Some things are more important than gold.
   d. Breakfast and lunch are important.

Cut out the cards and practice learning the words.

rainbow	important
surprised	daughter
beautiful	furniture

Imagine Learning®

Name: _____

The Fisherman and His Wife

Adapted by Eric Orton
Illustrated by Nate Baertsch
Lexile®: 400L, 315 words

A fisherman lived in a tiny cottage with his wife. One day the fisherman caught a beautiful golden fish.

"Please let me live," said the fish. The fisherman was surprised and dropped the fish. It swam away.

The fisherman told his wife about the talking fish. "That fish is magic!" said the wife. "Go back and wish for a mansion."

The fisherman returned to the sea. He called to the fish.

"What do you want?" the fish asked.

"My wife would like a mansion," replied the fisherman.

"I will grant her wish because you let me live," said the fish.

The fisherman went home. He was shocked to find a mansion where his cottage had been.

They were happy for many months. Then the wife wanted more. "Go ask the fish to make me the queen," she said.

The fisherman returned to the sea. He called to the fish.

"Now what do you want?" the fish asked.

"My wife wants you to make her the queen," replied the fisherman.

"I gave you a mansion!" said the fish. "But you set me free, so I will grant one last wish."

The fisherman returned home to find a grand palace. In a large room, his wife sat on a beautiful golden throne.

For many years they ruled happily, but then his wife wanted more. "Go tell the fish that I want to rule the world," said the wife.

The fisherman returned to the sea. He called to the fish.

Name: _____

"Why are you here again?" the fish asked.

"My wife would like to rule the world," replied the fisherman. The fish was angry. It realized they would always want more.

"Your wife is too greedy. I've turned your palace into a cave," said the fish. It shook its head and swam away.

And that is where the fisherman and his wife lived out the rest of their days.

| Accuracy: # of reading errors: _____ (Indep. = 0–7, Instr. = 8-16, Frust. = 17+) |
| Speed: To calculate: 18900 ÷ _____ (Reading time in seconds) = _____ WPM |

Transition Books: The Fisherman and His Wife
Copyright © Imagine Learning, Inc.

Name

The Fisherman and His Wife

Comprehension Questions

1. **What did the fisherman do with the golden fish?**
   a. dropped it in the water
   b. took it home to his wife
   c. put it in a cave
   d. ate it for dinner

2. **What was the wife's second wish?**
   a. to rule the world
   b. to have a mansion
   c. to live in a cave
   d. to be the queen

3. **Why did the fish turn the palace into a cave?**
   a. The fisherman's wife wished for too much.
   b. The fish liked the cave better than the palace.
   c. The palace was too big for the fisherman and his wife.
   d. The fisherman wanted to live closer to the sea.

4. **What lesson does this story teach?**
   a. Talking fish will grant wishes.
   b. It's easy to get a palace.
   c. Don't be greedy.
   d. Always wish for everything you want.

 **WORD CARDS**

Cut out the cards and practice learning the words.

fisherman	realized
angry	golden
mansion	cottage

Word Cards: The Fisherman and His Wife
Copyright © Imagine Learning, Inc.

 Imagine Learning®

Notes

Leveled Books Guide

About Leveled Books

Imagine Learning's Leveled Books provide literary and informational texts in a variety of genres at each reading level. Leveled books include narratives, myths, and plays, as well as biographies and informational texts that teach content from math, science, and social studies. Selections are paired: one text provides background knowledge for the other. Reading levels are determined by Lexile measures, and books are grouped into grades based on target Lexile measurements for each grade. The Leveled Book resources that support reading comprehension are:

- Leveled Book Texts and Comprehension Questions
- Graphic Organizers
- Reading Response Journals

Leveled Book Texts and Comprehension Questions

Resource Overview

Leveled Book Texts are printouts of the book cover and text. Each printout includes information for a thematically paired Leveled Book, Lexile measurement, and word count. Each Leveled Book text also includes an Oral Reading Fluency assessment box to evaluate students' oral reading ability.

Comprehension Question types for leveled books include literal, inferential, vocabulary, main idea, story map, author's purpose, intertextual, cause/effect, compare/contrast, and problem/solution. Each Comprehension Question sheet also includes vocabulary and glossary words used in the books. Answers to questions are located in the Leveled Books Answer Key.

How to Use This Resource in the Classroom

Whole class or small group reading

- Conduct a shared reading experience, inviting individual students to read segments of the story aloud.
- After reading a selection together, call on volunteers to connect the story to a personal experience, comment on his or her favorite part, or share what he or she has learned from the reading.

Partner Reading

- Select from (or allow students to select from) the following options to read aloud in pairs.
  - **Choral Reading:** Have students sit together and read the text aloud together.
  - **Echo Reading:** Have one partner read a line and have the other partner repeat the line. Alternate roles with each new paragraph.
  - **Taking Turns:** Have students take turns reading a sentence or paragraph at a time.
  - **Silent Reading:** Have partners read silently, sitting near one another so that they can ask each other for help when needed.
  - **Part Reading:** Have one partner read any narration, or any parts that aren't dialogue. Have the other partner read the characters' parts, using different voices for each character.
- **Partner Work:** Allow students to read the same book and then together work on Comprehension Questions, Graphic Organizers, or Reading Response Journals, or other extension projects that correlate to the story.
- **Read and Tell:** Select a section of text and have both partners read silently, signaling each other when they are finished. Then have partners turn their printout face down and designate one partner as listener and the other as teller. The teller retells as much of the reading as possible. When the teller has finished, the listener may add any additional information he or she remembers. Then both partners turn over the text and skim the selection for ideas or facts that they may have missed. Select a new section and have partners swap roles and repeat the process.

Oral Reading

- Use the Oral Reading Fluency assessment box at the bottom of each leveled text printout to evaluate a student's oral reading ability. Listen to a student read for one minute, count the student's reading errors, and then use the formulas displayed in the box at the bottom of the page. Formulas are based on counting

Imagine Learning®

errors that change grammar or distort meaning. Self corrections and mispronunciations of names are not counted as errors. Mistakes that should be counted as errors are:

Substitutions: Student replaces the word in the text with another word that doesn't mean the same thing (nonword substitutions are always counted as errors each time they are said).

Omissions: Student leaves out a word in the text.

Insertions: Student adds an extra word to the text.

In the example box below, taken from the article *Falling Rocks of Ice*, if students make four or fewer errors, they are reading at an independent level. Students can make as many as eleven errors and still read at an instructional level. More than twelve errors indicates a frustration level.

Accuracy: # of reading errors: _____ (Indep. = 0–4, Instr. = 5–11, Frust. = 12+)	
Speed: To calculate: 13260 ÷ _____ (Reading time in seconds) = _____ WPM	

Graphic Organizers

Resource Overview

Graphic organizers help students understand what they read by chunking information visually and showing relationships between ideas. Leveled Books include organizers that focus on crucial comprehension skills, such as main idea and supporting details, sequence of events, cause and effect, compare and contrast, story map, and more . Each organizer includes instructions and content specific to the leveled text it accompanies.

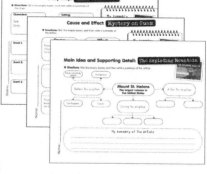

How to Use This Resource in the Classroom

- Have students follow the instructions on the printout, either independently or with a partner. After students complete the graphic organizer, evaluate their word or have partners compare and self-evaluate.

- Have a student put the Leveled Book printout and graphic organizer side by side. Work with the student to look for the clue words on the graphic organizer and highlight them in the Leveled Book. Have the student fill in the rest of the graphic organizer by searching for the words in the text that support the clue words.

- Model how to turn the information from the graphic organizer into sentences and how to order the sentences into a summary. Have students then do the same independently. For an extension, have the student add one specific detail after each summary sentence.

Reading Response Journals

Resource Overview

Reading Response Journals help students show comprehension by connecting the story to personal experiences or ideas. Each journal page includes two writing prompts.

How to Use This Resource in the Classroom

- Have students choose one of the prompts to answer in a written paragraph with complete sentences. Encourage students to use words from the Words You Might Use section for language support.

- Clarify difficult vocabulary, provide helpful ideas, or model the activity to ensure comprehension. If there are issues with the student's response, such as lack of details, or not using key vocabulary, do one of the following:

  - Help the student brainstorm how the story connects to his or her everyday life.

  - Help the student identify additional vocabulary that could enrich the writing piece.

- Extend the reading experience by having the student prepare for an imaginary interview with the main character of the story. Have the student write five questions he or she would like to ask. Have the student pair with another student to role play the interview. Have the students use the reading response journal to record their partner's responses.

- Have the students create an event to add to the beginning or the end of the story. Have the students write about the new events in detail in the Response Journal.

Leveled Books Answer Key

Book Title	Q1	Q2	Q3
Grade 2			
Hide and Seek	b	c	a
Petroglyphs	c	c	b
Museums	c	a	c
Symbols and Secrets	a	c	a
Don't Eat Me	a	b	a
Tarantula Defense	b	c	a
A Party Surprise	c	a	b
World of Celebrations	c	b	b
I Don't Understand	b	b	c
Don't Fence Me in	c	b	c
Falling Rocks of Ice	c	a	c
Lost	a	a	c
The Can Dance	a	b	a
Ben's Big Ideas	a	b	c
Weightless in Space	c	c	b
Sir Isaac Newton	a	b	c
Grade 3			
Museums (Advanced)	b	b	a
Symbols and Secrets (Advanced)	b	a	c
Curtains Up	a	a	c
The Case of Missing Manny	a	c	a
Hide and Seek (Advanced)	a	a	c
Petroglyphs (Advanced)	b	b	a
A Party Surprise (Advanced)	c	a	b
World of Celebrations (Advanced)	b	a	b
Rainforest Explorer	b	a	b
Searching	a	b	a
The Record Breakers	c	a	c
Picture This	b	c	c
Davy Crockett: Larger than Life	b	b	c
Sally Ann Thunder Ann Whirlwind	a	b	a
Board Sports	b	c	a
Inventions	c	a	b
Your Own Secret Army	a	c	a
Stopping the Killers	b	c	b

Name: _____

Hide and Seek

Lesson 55

Paired with *Petroglyphs*

Written by Rebecca Suares
Illustrated by Jim Madsen

Lexile®: 480L, 276 words

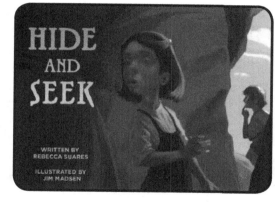

I was scooting on my belly under the brush. I had to reach the car before Josh found me. If I could touch it, I'd win the game.

I could hear Josh's footsteps just a few feet away from me. If I made any noise at all, he'd find me. I'd be out of the game.

"I can hear you, Sandy, and I'm going to find you," I heard Josh holler.

As I snaked away from Josh, I made a wrong turn. A solid wall of rock blocked my way.

Quickly, I slid along the wall. There had to be a way around it somewhere. Or maybe there was a way through it.

Off to my left, I could barely make out a dark line on the rock. I inched over to it, hoping it was a crack that I could hide in. Josh would never find me there.

I'd wait for him to pass, and then I'd dash for the car before he could find me. I slithered over to the line.

Sure enough, it was a narrow crack in the rock. I planned to hide for a few seconds until Josh passed by, but then I saw something.

Wow! It wasn't just a crack in the rock. It was a secret entrance to an ancient room!

The rock walls were covered with strange drawings. I forgot all about the game and yelled "Hey, Josh! Come over here. Look what I found! This is so cool! "

"Awesome!" he gasped as he wiggled through the crack. "They're petroglyphs, Sandy. Let's show Mom and Dad."

"Oh, and by the way—you're out. I win the game."

Accuracy: # of reading errors: _____ (Indep. = 0–6, Instr. = 7–14, Frust. = 15+)
Speed: To calculate: 16560 ÷ _____ (Reading time in seconds) = _____ WPM

Name: _____

Hide and Seek

Lesson 55
Paired with *Petroglyphs*

Discovery Story Vocabulary	hide and seek, entrance, ancient
Glossary Words	ancient, petroglyphs, you're out

Question Type	Question
Literal	Where did she have to go to win? a. the cliff b. the car c. the bush
Vocabulary	Why is the story called Hide and Seek? a. Both kids would hide, and the parents would find them. b. The kids were trying to find hidden pictures. c. One kid would hide, and the other would find her.
Inferential	Josh said he won the game because he found _____. a. Sandy before she got to the car b. a rock wall with a crack c. petroglyphs on the rock

Name: _____

Story Map: Hide and Seek

✳ Directions: Fill in the empty boxes, and then write a summary of the story.

Characters:
Josh
Sandy

Setting:

Event 1:

Event 2:

Event 3:

My summary
of the story

HIDE
AND
SEEK

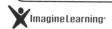

Graphic Organizer: Hide and Seek
Copyright © Imagine Learning, Inc.

Name: _____

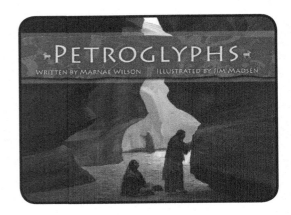

Petroglyphs

Lesson 56

Paired with *Hide and Seek*

Written by Marnae Wilson
Illustrated by Jim Madsen

Lexile®: 450L, 108 words

What if you had a great story to write, but you had no paper or pencil? How would you save your story?

Many years ago, people drew pictures on rock to tell about their lives.

They would show what they did every day. They would draw pictures of their families.

They would draw their animals.

These pictures on rock are called petroglyphs. They are found all over the world.

Some are clear and easy to see. But some have been damaged by weather.

And some have been damaged by people touching or writing on them.

We must protect petroglyphs. They tell us about people who lived long ago.

Accuracy: # of reading errors: _____ (Indep. = 0–2, Instr. = 3–5, Frust. = 6+)
Speed: To calculate: 6480 ÷ _____ (Reading time in seconds) = _____ WPM

Leveled Books: Petroglyphs
Copyright © Imagine Learning, Inc.

Name: _____

Petroglyphs
Lesson 56
Paired with *Hide and Seek*

Discover Story Vocabulary	petroglyphs, history
Glossary Words	damaged, protect

Question Type	Question
Main Idea	What is this article mostly about? a. dangerous weather b. wild animals c. rock drawings
Cause	What causes damage to petroglyphs? a. pictures b. stories c. weather
Antonym	What is an antonym for the word "protect"? a. save b. damage c. petroglyphs

Name: _____

Response Journal

Think about the article **Petroglyphs**.

Write about a time that you found something interesting. Describe what you found. Where did you find it? How did you find it?

OR

Does this article make you think of something you've read, heard, or seen? Write about it.

_____

_____

_____

_____

_____

_____

_____

_____

_____

_____

_____

WORDS YOU MIGHT USE

This article reminds me of...   discovered   location
I remember when...   unusual   surprised

Imagine Learning

Name: _____

Museums

Lesson 57

Paired with *Symbols and Secrets*

Written by Anna Matola
Illustrated by Maryn Roos

Lexile®: 630L, 72 words

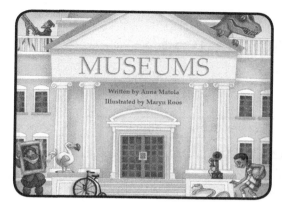

Museums have lots of different things in them that teach us about the world we live in.

There are art museums, sports museums, and insect museums. There are even museums of money.

Some museums let kids explore how things work.

Many museums have unusual objects.

Often museums have things from the past.

And some museums have amazing art.

Museums are fun places to visit, and you can learn a lot too!

Accuracy: # of reading errors: _____ (Indep. = 0–1, Instr. = 2–4, Frust. = 5+)
Speed: To calculate: 4320 ÷ _____ (Reading time in seconds) = _____ WPM

 Imagine Learning®

Leveled Books: Museums
Copyright © Imagine Learning, Inc.

Name: _____

Museums

Lesson 57
Paired with *Symbols and Secrets*

Discover Story Vocabulary	display, unusual
Glossary Words	unusual, amazing

Question Type	Question
Inferential	What might be in an art museum? a. machines b. insects c. paintings
Author's Purpose	Why did the author write this article? a. to tell about different kinds of museums b. to show where museums are located c. to teach about art in museums
Literal	What do museums teach us about? a. the schools we go to b. our families c. the world we live in

Name: _____

Main Idea and Supporting Detail:

❋ Directions: Fill in the empty boxes with information about museums. Then write a summary of the article.

Museums

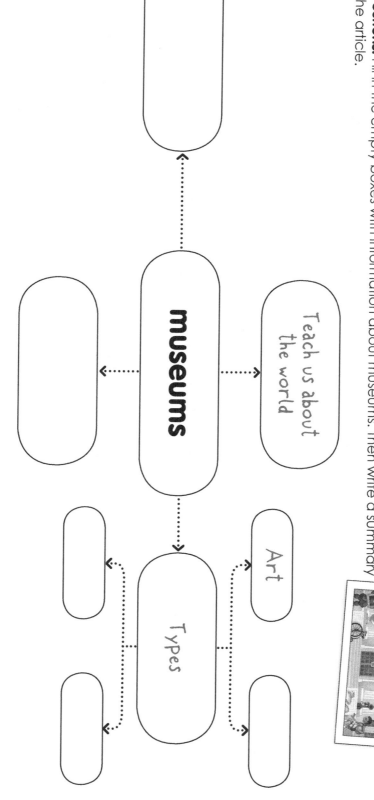

museums

Teach us about the world

Types

Art

My summary of the article

Name: _____

Symbols and Secrets

Lesson 58

Paired with *Museums*

Written by Anna Matola
Illustrated by Nate Baertsch

Lexile®: 510L, 325 words

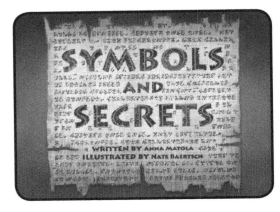

"And this symbol often stood for hidden treasure," said the museum guide.

"I think I've seen something like that before," whispered Mike to Kayla. "It was at my grandpa's house."

"No way! Do you think there's a hidden treasure in his house?" asked Kayla.

"Let's go see," Mike suggested as they hurried from the museum.

"Grandpa, we think your house has a hidden treasure. Can we look for it?" asked Mike, when his grandpa came to the door.

"Sure." Grandpa smiled. "But only if you'll let me help."

They looked in every room of the house, but there was no symbol and no hidden treasure.

"Let's try the attic," suggested Grandpa. "Maybe the treasure is up there."

They looked in every corner of the attic. No symbol. No hidden treasure.

"I'm tired," groaned Mike as he headed toward the stairs. "Maybe I was wrong about that symbol. Why would there be a hidden treasure in your house, anyway?"

"Wait!" said Kayla. "Look at that brick at the bottom of the chimney! Isn't that a symbol? Maybe the treasure is hidden in the chimney!"

Mike pulled on the brick, and it moved a little. Suddenly, part of the wall slid open, showing the top of a staircase.

"Wow," whispered Mike as they peered into the dark passage. "I wonder if there really is a treasure down there."

"There's only one way to find out!" said Kayla as she bounded down the staircase.

Name: _____

Mike followed her nervously.

"Hey! Look over here!" shouted Kayla, dusting the cobwebs off an antique box. "I think we found it!"

Mike and Kayla's discovery made history!

Mike and Kayla were heroes because they returned the jewel to the museum. "We have been searching for this jewel for a long time," said the museum guide. "Thank you."

"No problem," said Mike. "I wonder what we'll find next!"

Accuracy: # of reading errors: _____ (Indep. = 0–7, Instr. = 8–16, Frust. = 17+)
Speed: To calculate: 19500 ÷ _____ (Reading time in seconds) = _____ WPM

 ImagineLearning®

Leveled Books: Symbols and Secrets

Name: _____

Symbols and Secrets

Lesson 58
Paired with *Museums*

Discover Story Vocabulary	symbol, guide, nervously
Glossary Words	guide, treasure, attic, symbol, nervously, discovery

Question Type	Question
Setting	What was the setting for this story? a. Grandpa's house b. Kayla's house c. Mike's house
Literal	Where did Kayla find the symbol? a. on the stairs b. on the door c. on the chimney
Intertextual	*Symbols and Secrets* and *Museums* have something in common. They **both** _____. a. talk about museums b. describe kids solving mysteries c. discuss different kinds of art collections

Name: _____

Response Journal

Think about the story **Symbols and Secrets**.

Describe Kayla. Describe Mike. How are they alike and how are they different?

OR

Does this story make you think about something you've read, heard, or seen? Write about it.

_____

_____

_____

_____

_____

_____

_____

_____

_____

_____

WORDS YOU MIGHT USE

I read a book where...	brave	leader
I saw a movie where...	adventure	mystery
nervous	determined	

Name: _____

Don't Eat Me!

Lesson 59

Paired with *Tarantula Defense*

Written by Daniel Rietz
Illustrated by Jim Madsen

Lexile®: 570L, 134 words

Some animals eat other animals. So most animals have ways to protect themselves. They run, or hide, or fight.

Run

Some animals move fast to get away from enemies. For example, a gazelle can run as fast as a car.

Ostriches run very fast, too. Animals that run fast are hard to catch and eat.

Hide

Some animals are hard to see. A snowshoe rabbit is white, so it can hide in the snow.

An interesting insect called a walking stick looks just like a twig. These animals can hide from enemies.

Fight

Some animals can fight to stay safe. For example, spiders and snakes bite to kill other animals.

Lions and bears have strong teeth and claws to fight with. Many animals stay safe because they run, hide, or fight.

| Accuracy: # of reading errors: _____ (Indep. = 0–3, Instr. = 4–7, Frust. = 8+) |
| Speed: To calculate: 8040 ÷ _____ (Reading time in seconds) = _____ WPM |

Name: _____

Don't Eat Me!

Lesson 59
Paired with *Tarantula Defense*

Discover Story Vocabulary	develop, protect
Glossary Words	enemies

Question Type	Question
Main Idea	What is the main idea of this article? a. Animals run, hide, or fight to protect themselves. b. The snowshoe rabbit is very hard to see when it snows. c. The best way for animals to protect themselves is to run as fast as a car.
Literal	What kind of protection does an ostrich use? a. It attacks with its beak. b. It runs very fast. c. It hides near trees.
Author's Purpose	Why does the author use headings in this article? a. to help you see the important ideas b. to make the article long enough to fit on the page c. to make the pictures more important

Name: _____

Main Idea and Supporting Detail:

Don't Eat Me!

❋ Directions: Fill in the empty boxes, and then write a summary of the article.

Ways animals defend themselves

run → **example** → ostriches

→ **example**

→ **example**

My summary of the article

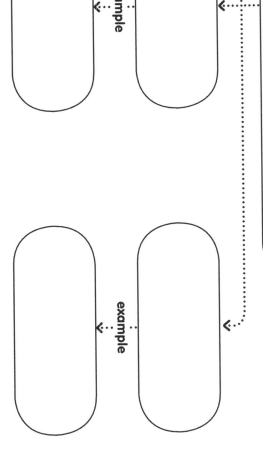

Graphic Organizer: Don't Eat Me!
Copyright © Imagine Learning, Inc.

 Imagine Learning®

Name: _____

Tarantula Defense

Lesson 60

Paired with *Don't Eat Me!*

Written by Daniel Rietz

Illustrated by Jim Madsen

Lexile®: 490L, 79 words

Animals run, hide, or fight to stay safe.

Tarantulas can't run or hide easily. But they can fight.

The spider's belly hairs are a secret weapon.

They are coated with poison. These hairs fly into an enemy's eyes.

The enemy tries to get the hairs out. And the tarantula gets away.

So if you look at a tarantula and see a bald spot on its belly, it may have been in a fight for its life.

And it won.

Accuracy: # of reading errors: _____ (Indep. = 0–2, Instr. = 3–4, Frust. = 5+)

Speed: To calculate: 4740 ÷ _____ (Reading time in seconds) = _____ WPM

Name: _____

Tarantula Defense

Lesson 60
Paired with *Don't Eat Me!*

Classroom Activities

Discover Story Vocabulary	defense, weapon
Glossary Words	weapon, coated

Question Type	Question
Literal	What is the tarantula's secret weapon? a. places to hide b. poisonous belly hairs c. enemies
Vocabulary	Read this sentence from the article: "[The hairs] are <u>coated</u> with poison." What does "coated" mean? a. kept warm b. moved very fast c. covered all over
Inferential	Why did the enemy let the tarantula go? a. Because the enemy had poison in its eyes. b. Because the enemy is afraid of the tarantula. c. Because the poison killed the enemy.

Comprehension Questions: Tarantula Defense
Copyright © Imagine Learning, Inc.

Name: _____

Response Journal

Tarantula Defense
WRITTEN BY DANIEL RIETZ · ILLUSTRATED BY JIM MADSEN

Think about the article **Tarantula Defense.**

Write about an experience you had with an animal or an insect. Describe what happened. Where did it happen? What did you learn from the experience?

OR

Does this article make you think about something in your own life? Does it make you think of something you've read or seen? Write about it.

_____

_____

_____

_____

_____

_____

_____

_____

WORDS YOU MIGHT USE

This article reminds me of...	dangerous	caught
I remember when...	watched	chased
interesting	attacked	
discovered	protect	

Imagine Learning®

Response Journal: Tarantula Defense
Copyright © Imagine Learning, Inc.

Name: _____

A Party Surprise

Lesson 61

Paired with *World of Celebrations*

Written by Marnae Wilson
Illustrated by Jim Madsen

Lexile®: 500L, 356 words

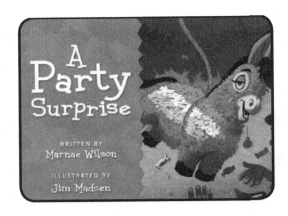

Whack! The swinging piñata is hit hard. Everyone laughs and cheers. A piñata is a hollow shape that is filled with candy. When someone breaks it open, everyone gets a treat.

You can make your own piñata. You must first get some paper and a balloon. Newspaper is inexpensive and easy to use. Then decide what balloon to use. Now you're ready to begin.

First, mix flour and water until it's thick and smooth. That's your paste. Then blow up the balloon. Next, tear the paper into short strips. Finally, dip each strip into the paste and lay it on the balloon. Smooth it down with your hands. Cover the whole balloon with the paper strips. But make sure you leave an opening at the top.

Now, let the paper get very dry. When the paper feels hard, pop the balloon. Surprise! You have an empty ball.

It's time to decorate the empty ball. You can use ribbons, paper, or feathers. You can glue on anything that is bright and colorful. Decorate it any way you want.

Now, fill your piñata with candy, treats, or small gifts. Small, hard candy that is wrapped works best. It doesn't break easily when the piñata is hit. It doesn't get dirty when it lands on the ground. Make sure there is enough for everyone to get a piece.

Your piñata is finally ready. Now it's time for a party! Hang your piñata from a tree. Cover someone's eyes with a cloth. Then, let the person try to hit the piñata with a stick. One hit probably won't break the piñata, so let people take turns

Name: _____

others might only get a piece or two. But everyone will have fun scrambling for treats.

Piñatas are fun to make and break. They have been popular in Mexico for a long time. But Mexico isn't the only country that plays with piñatas. They are fun for parties all over the world.

Accuracy: # of reading errors: _____ (Indep. = 0–7, Instr. = 8–18, Frust. = 19+)
Speed: To calculate: 21360 ÷ _____ (Reading time in seconds) = _____ WPM

 Imagine Learning®

Leveled Books: A Party Surprise
Copyright © Imagine Learning, Inc.

Name: _____

A Party Surprise

Lesson 61

Paired with *World of Celebrations*

Discover Story Vocabulary	piñata, Mexico
Glossary Words	decorate, piñata, popular

Question Type	Question
Main Idea	What would be another good title for this article? a. *Party Ideas for Babies* b. *Candy for Your Party!* a. *How to Make a Piñata*
Vocabulary	Read this sentence from the article: "[Piñatas] have been <u>popular</u> in Mexico for a long time." What does the word "popular" mean? a. liked by many people b. kept away from children c. found in Mexico
Cause	What causes the strips of paper to get hard? a. They pop. b. They dry. c. They are torn.

Comprehension Questions: A Party Surprise
Copyright © Imagine Learning, Inc.

Name: _____

Sequence:

A Party Surprise

✱ Directions: Fill in the steps below to describe how to make a piñata.

1: Get your materials together: flour, water, newspaper, and a balloon.

2:

3: Tear the newspaper into strips, then dip the strips one by one into the paste.

4:

5: Let the newspaper strips dry completely. Now you have an empty ball.

6:

My summary of the article

Graphic Organizer: A Party Surprise
Copyright © Imagine Learning, Inc.

Imagine Learning®

Name: _____

World of Celebrations

Lesson 62
Paired with *A Party Surprise*
Written by Marnae Wilson
Illustrated by Jim Madsen

Lexile®: 570L, 545 words

All over the world, people get together to celebrate. They celebrate birthdays. They celebrate religious holidays. They celebrate national holidays. And each culture celebrates in a different way. Some people make special holiday foods. Some wear special holiday clothes. Some have special holiday parties. Here's a look at a few celebrations around the world.

Kauai is one of the Hawaiian Islands in the Pacific Ocean.

In Kauai, people have had fun at the Coconut Festival for many years. Coconuts grow at the top of tall, thin palm trees. Every part of the coconut tree is useful. The trunk can be used for wood. The leaves can be used to make mats and roofs. The nut can be eaten or pressed to get oil. The husk and shell can be burned for fuel.

During the festival, Hawaiians have coconut contests. Who can be the first one to the top of a coconut palm? Who can crack a coconut open the fastest? Who can make the best food using coconuts? Kids paint them. Teenagers play ball with them. Men and women make clothes out of their leaves. And performers dance and sing. Coconuts are very important to Hawaiians, so at the Coconut Festival, people celebrate coconuts.

Just south of Hawaii is the equator. Following the equator east leads to the African continent. The Ivory Coast is located there.

Every year people in the villages make masks. Some of the masks look like animal heads. Some look like scary faces. In November, the villagers celebrate the Festival of Masks. They wear their masks and dance. Huge drums boom the rhythm. Which dancer moves the most like an animal? Which mask is best? The most skilled dancers in each village get to dance at the national Festival of Masks.

Following the prime meridian north from the Ivory Coast leads to England, part of the European continent.

Name: _____

After a cold winter, the English celebrate the coming of spring on May 1. Each community has its own party. They decorate the streets with flowers and greenery. Often, they put up a maypole with wide ribbons hanging from it. Dancers weave the ribbons as they move around the pole. Other groups dance through the streets. Many people wear white. Girls carry flowers and put flowers in their hair. May Day is a time for love and joy.

East of the European continent is the Asian continent. Thailand is at the south end of the Asian continent.

Every April 13, Thai people celebrate the new year with the Water Festival. This festival is a time to honor older relatives. Young people pour water over their grandparents' hands as a sign of respect.

But the Water Festival is mostly for fun. For three days, people play with water. They throw cups of water at people walking by. They shoot water guns at their friends. They soak their neighbors with garden hoses. All over the country, people have huge water fights. April is the hottest month of the year in Thailand. The Water Festival is a fun way to cool down.

Celebrations happen all over the world on all different continents. People eat special meals. They give gifts. And, they have parties. Celebrations are a time to remember traditions and a time to have fun.

Accuracy: # of reading errors: _____ (Indep. = 0–11, Instr. = 12–27, Frust. = 28+)
Speed: To calculate: 32700 ÷ _____ (Reading time in seconds) = _____ WPM

Name: _____

World of Celebrations

Lesson 62

Paired with *A Party Surprise*

Discovery Story Vocabulary	celebration, continent
Glossary Words	culture, celebrations, festival, continent

Question Type	Question
Intertextual	How are *A Party Surprise* and this article alike? a. They both tell how to make something for a party. b. They both tell what people in Mexico do at parties. c. They both tell about celebrations.
Author's Purpose	The author included maps in the article because _____. a. she wanted the reader to plan a trip around the world b. she wanted to show where in the world the different countries were c. she wanted to make her article longer
Contrast	**Thailand** **Both** **England** celebrate with water / celebrate in the spring Which of the following goes in the empty circle? a. celebrate with coconuts b. celebrate with ribbons c. celebrate with masks

Name: _____

Response Journal

Think about the article **World of Celebrations**.

Write about a special celebration you have in your family or in your culture. How do you prepare for the celebration? What do you do at the celebration? Who comes to celebrate with you?

OR

Write about your favorite celebration. Why do you like it? Describe what you do at this celebration.

_____

_____

_____

_____

_____

_____

_____

_____

_____

_____

WORDS YOU MIGHT USE

experience	relatives	recipes
competition	neighbors	delicious
parade	laughter	aromas
fireworks	excitement	

 Imagine Learning®

I Don't Understand

Lesson 63

Paired with *Don't Fence Me In*

Written by David Pali
Illustrated by Jim Madsen

Lexile®: 500L, 339 words

Blowing his whistle, Mr. Morgan signaled that it was time for PE to start. Ricardo hated PE. He didn't know the rules for American football and basketball. So he always looked silly.

"Settle down, you guys, or you'll be in hot water," Mr. Morgan demanded.

What did "hot water" have to do with PE? Ricardo wondered.

Being new wasn't working out very well. Every day the kids at school made fun of him. He didn't dress like they did, and he couldn't understand what they were saying.

Just yesterday a couple of boys had pointed at him and said, "What's with the shoes, dude?" He'd looked around him and couldn't see anything "with" his shoes. What were they talking about?

Then there was the money. How many nickels made a quarter? How many dimes were in a dollar? How much American money was a quetzal worth?

So now it was time for PE again. Whenever they chose teams, Ricardo was last to be picked. He just couldn't figure out how the games worked, so the kids didn't want him on their team.

As he trudged over to his group, he heard Mr. Morgan announce that this morning they would be playing soccer. Soccer? Ricardo knew how to play soccer! He played it every day. They called it "football" in Guatemala.

His team wasn't very good at soccer, though. They couldn't move the ball down the field, let alone score a goal. Good thing the other team was just as bad. And, of course, no one ever sent the ball his way. They didn't even know he could play.

Then, just by chance, the ball came spinning towards Ricardo. With a flick of his foot, he had it under control. Quick as lightning he was speeding down the field, dribbling the ball easily, avoiding all the players who tried to block him.

Name: _____

Goal! Ricardo smiled as his team ran up to him.

"Cool shot!" they said.

"That was awesome."

Now those were English words that he could understand!

Accuracy: # of reading errors: _____ (Indep. = 0–7, Instr. = 8–17, Frust. = 18+)
Speed: To calculate: 20340 ÷ _____ (Reading time in seconds) = _____ WPM

I Don't Understand

Lesson 63
Paired with *Don't Fence Me In*

Discover Story Vocabulary	signal, under control, avoid
Glossary Words	signaled, choose teams, under control

Question Type	Question
Inferential	What is true about Ricardo? a. He likes to play basketball. b. He's not happy in his new country. c. He gets to choose his own team.
Vocabulary	Read this sentence from the story: "Quick as lightening he was speeding down the field, dribbling the ball easily, avoiding all the players who tried to block him." What does "avoiding" mean? a. moving closer to b. staying away from c. touching
Problem	What is Ricardo's problem during the soccer game? a. All the other kids on his team are good soccer players. b. He is wearing the wrong clothes to play soccer. c. No one will pass him the ball.

Name: _____

Story Map: I Don't Understand

✳ Directions: Fill in the empty boxes, and then write a summary of the story.

Characters:

Setting:

Problem:

Trying to get used to life in a new country

Plot:

Solution:

My summary of the story

I DON'T UNDERSTAND

Don't Fence Me In

Lesson 64

Paired with *I Don't Understand*

Written by David Pali
Illustrated by Maryn Roos

Lexile®: 480L, 112 words

Have you ever wished you had more space in your house or yard?

All over the world, people have wanted their own land. So they move to new places to get it.

They move to new cities. They move to new countries.

When America was a new country, some people came to get land and to have more freedom.

Soon it became crowded. So people moved west.

These pioneers started new farms and towns.

Now people live all over America. But they still want more space.

Maybe someday families who want more space will move again—perhaps to the moon or another planet. Maybe you'll be one of the new space pioneers.

Accuracy: # of reading errors: _____ (Indep. = 0–2, Instr. = 3–6, Frust. = 7+)
Speed: To calculate: 6720 ÷ _____ (Reading time in seconds) = _____ WPM

Name: _____

Don't Fence Me In

Lesson 64
Paired with *I Don't Understand*

Classroom Activities

| Discover Story Vocabulary | freedom, pioneer |
| Glossary Words | freedom, pioneers |

Question Type	Question
Cause	What caused people to come to America? a. They wanted to live in a wilderness. b. They wanted to get away from their families and friends. c. They wanted to get land and have more freedom.
Main Idea	What is another good title for this article? a. "Exploring New Planets" b. "Finding a Better Place to Live" c. "How Towns Grow into Cities"
Intertextual	In *I Don't Understand*, Ricardo was like the pioneers because he _____. a. liked to play soccer b. left England c. moved to a new place

 Imagine Learning®

Comprehension Questions: Don't Fence Me In
Copyright © Imagine Learning, Inc.

99

Name: _____

Response Journal

Think about the article **Don't Fence Me In**.

Do you ever feel like you need more space? When do you feel crowded? What do you do when you feel crowded?

OR

Does this article make you think about something in your own life? Does it make you think of something you've read, heard, or seen? Write about it.

_____

_____

_____

_____

_____

_____

_____

_____

WORDS YOU MIGHT USE

This article reminds me of...   crowded   businesses
family   wilderness   travel
freedom   country

Response Journal: Don't Fence Me In

Name: _____

Falling Rocks of Ice

Lesson 65

Paired with *Lost*

Written by Marnae Wilson
Illustrated by Alisa Haggard

Lexile®: 540L, 221 words

Clouds

You've seen pictures of big white clouds. They look as soft as pillows. But watch out! They could mean trouble.

There are three main kinds of clouds. Cirrus clouds are very high and stretch across the sky in long bands. They are a sign of good weather.

Stratus clouds look like a sheet of gray fog. They don't hold much water, but a light rain might fall from them.

Cumulus clouds are tall and puffy. If the wind picks up and it gets cold, they turn dark. Then they may be a sign of danger. They can produce hail.

Hail

Let's look at hail. Hail is ice that falls from cumulus clouds. What makes hail fall?

Hail starts as very cold rain. When the wind is strong inside clouds, the rain doesn't fall. It blows around and around.

Soon the rain freezes into tiny pieces of ice. Then the pieces of ice hit more rain drops. The drops freeze onto the ice, and the hail gets bigger and bigger.

The ice gets too heavy for the wind to hold, and it falls from the clouds. Big balls of hail are like rocks. They can ruin crops and kill animals.

Scientists can't stop hail, but they can warn people before the rocks of ice start to fall.

Accuracy: # of reading errors: _____ (Indep. = 0–4, Instr. = 5–11, Frust. = 12+)
Speed: To calculate: 13260 ÷ _____ (Reading time in seconds) = _____ WPM

Name: _____

Falling Rocks of Ice

Lesson 65
Paired with *Lost*

Discover Story Vocabulary	smile, band, warn
Glossary Words	trouble, bands, like a sheet of gray fog, hail, warn

Question Type	Question
Literal	The three main kinds of clouds are _____. a. hail, rain, and snow b. big, fluffy, and thin c. cirrus, stratus, and cumulus
Compare	What belongs in the empty box? **What do the clouds look like?** | Cirrus	Cumulus
long, thin bands	| a. tall and puffy b. thin bands c. sheet of gray fog
Cause	Hail falls because drops of ice _____. a. turn dark b. become fluffy c. get heavy

Comprehension Questions: Falling Rocks of Ice
Copyright © Imagine Learning, Inc.

Name: _____

Response Journal

Think about the article **Falling Rocks of Ice**.

Write about an experience you have had with the weather. Was it a storm or just terribly hot? Where were you? How did you feel? What happened?

OR

Does this article make you think about something you've read, heard, or seen? Write about it.

_____

_____

_____

_____

_____

_____

_____

_____

_____

WORDS YOU MIGHT USE

This article reminds me of...	interesting	thunder
I remember when...	miserable	trouble
scared	lightning	shelter

 ImagineLearning®

Name: _____

Lost

Lesson 66

Paired with *Falling Rocks of Ice*

Written by Marnae Wilson
Illustrated by Jim Madsen

Lexile®: 460L, 341 words

How could I be lost? I thought camp was just around this hill. Now what should I do?

A drop of rain hit me on the nose. Just what I needed—a storm. And I thought those big puffy clouds were pretty! What else could go wrong?

I started to look around for someplace to wait out the storm. Before long, someone would realize I was gone and come to find me.

More rain drops. If I didn't hurry, I'd be cold and wet, besides being lost. Maybe I could stay dry under a tree. But what if lightning struck the tree? I'd be toast.

I decided my best chance to stay dry was to sit under an overhanging rock. As I crouched under the rock, I started looking around to see if I could find the way back to camp.

Was that something moving over there? Did I see eyes squinting from under that bush? I grabbed a big stick with one hand and a rock with the other.

Kneeling, I stared at the bush. Something was staring back at me, and then it started to move. It looked like a big, gray, mangy dog. But it had its teeth bared and was growling. I realized then that I was in deep trouble. It was a wolf.

The wolf slowly crept closer, spit dripping from its mouth as it snarled. I squeezed my stick and rock to keep my hands from shaking, and then I waved my weapons and yelled as loud as I could.

No luck. The wolf crouched low to the ground, ready to attack.

Suddenly, a baseball hit the wolf on the head! Then another ball bounced down next to the wolf.

Then another, and another. Wait. Those baseballs were actually hail. Huge hailstones were pounding everywhere.

With a yelp, the wolf turned and ran. "All right!" I shouted, as I threw my stick and rock down.

A few minutes later the hail stopped, and I heard voices calling my name. "Here I am," I yelled.

Accuracy: # of reading errors: _____ (Indep. = 0–7, Instr. = 8–17, Frust. = 18+)
Speed: To calculate: 20460 ÷ _____ (Reading time in seconds) = _____ WPM

Name: _____

Classroom Activities

Lost

Lesson 66
Paired with *Falling Rocks of Ice*

Discover Story Vocabulary	narrow, stare
Glossary Words	stared, attack, all right

Question Type	Question
Problem	What problem did the boy in this story have? a. He was lost. b. He lost his dog. c. He lost his money.
Cause	Why did the boy get under a rock? a. It started to rain and he wanted to stay dry. b. He thought it would be easier for his friends to find him. c. He wanted to hide from any wild animals.
Plot	What happened right before the hail started to fall? a. The boy fell on the wolf. b. The boy got lost in the forest. c. The wolf moved closer to the boy.

Name: _____

Story Map: Lost

Directions: Fill in the empty boxes, and then write a summary of the story.

Characters:

Setting:

Problem:
The boy is lost.

Plot:

Solution:

My Summary of the story

Name: _____

The Can Dance

Lesson 67

Paired with *Ben's Big Ideas*

Written and Illustrated by Maryn Roos

Lexile®: 530L, 523 words

Right now there are hundreds of people beyond that curtain. There are millions more watching by television. And all of them are waiting for me to sing. I've always dreamed of being on TV. But how did I get here? Well, it all started when...

I was teaching my pet duck, Stumpy, to dance. We were listening to the latest Kayzha album. In the CD booklet, Kayzha wrote about her charity work. She included a list of ways to volunteer and help people. I decided I wanted to make a difference.

One idea was to collect canned foods and donate the cans to a local food bank. The food is used to help feed people who don't have enough to eat. My dad helped me pick out cans from our kitchen. Stumpy wanted to share his canned worms. Don't worry! Those stayed on our shelf.

I couldn't feed many people by myself. So, I decided to organize a food drive.

I made a list of everyone who volunteered to help. I divided us into four teams: the Red, Blue, Yellow, and Plaid Teams. We would compete to see who could collect the most cans. The losing teams would treat the winning team to a barbeque.

I assigned each team a different section of town. They would knock on doors and ask people to donate cans of food.

Everyone found ways to get people's attention. My cousins decorated their cart. It looked like a giant can-eating monster. My friends Matt and Casey sang funny songs. I took Stumpy with me. And we sang and danced.

One house on my list was having a big party. Everyone came out to watch me and Stumpy perform. They filled my wagon with cans. Then one of the women introduced herself.

"I work in the city on the Johnny Holliday Show," she said. "Would you and Stumpy like to do your act on TV?"

How could I say no? Stumpy's quack sounded like a happy "Yes!" He loves the spotlight.

Stumpy, my dad, and I went to the city. We toured the television studio. I saw the cameras and the sets. I got to meet the other guests for that night's show. And guess what? Would you believe Kayzha was going to be on the show too? I almost fainted.

I was nervous to be on TV. But then Stumpy tried to eat Johnny Holliday's coat buttons, and that made me laugh. Mr. Holliday told jokes and asked about my can drive. He offered to double the amount of cans I already had. My team would win for sure!

And now here I am on a national television show. I am singing and dancing with my pet duck in front of millions. Kayzha is even singing with us! It is a dream come true—at least for me. I think Stumpy dreams of fat, juicy bugs.

It all started with a few cans from the cupboard. It ended with thousands of pounds of food collected to help fight hunger. It is amazing how small beginnings can lead to great things—things even more amazing than a dancing duck.

Accuracy: # of reading errors: _____ (Indep. = 0–10, Instr. = 11–26, Frust. = 27+)
Speed: To calculate: 31380 ÷ _____ (Reading time in seconds) = _____ WPM

 ImagineLearning®

Name: _____

The Can Dance
Lesson 67
Paired with *Ben's Big Ideas*

Discover Story Vocabulary	charity work, donation, volunteer
Glossary Words	donate, assigned, introduced

Question Type	Question
Character	Which of the following phrases best describes the main character? a. She helped others. b. She was a famous TV host. c. She sold cans.
Solution	The girl had a problem. She couldn't feed all the people who needed food by herself. How did she solve her problem? a. She got her dad to pick out cans from the kitchen. b. She got other people to help collect cans of food. c. She got Kazhya to ask people for cans on the radio.
Inferential	Read this sentence from the story: "One idea was to collect canned foods and donate the cans to a local food bank." A food bank is a place where _____. a. hungry people can go to get food b. poor people get money c. kids put money into a special account

Name: _____

Response Journal

Think about the story **The Can Dance**.

Write about the main character. Describe her to someone else. Use examples and details to support what you say about her.

OR

Does this story make you think about something in your own life? Does it make you think of something you've read or seen? Write about it.

_____

_____

_____

_____

_____

_____

_____

_____

_____

_____

WORDS YOU MIGHT USE

talented	leader	caring
funny	hardworking	friendly
creative	different	popular

Name: _____

Ben's Big Ideas

Lesson 68

Paired with *The Can Dance*

Written and illustrated by Maryn Roos

Lexile®: 530L, 324 words

Benjamin Franklin is an important person in history. He was born in colonial America. Franklin tried to make his community a better place. Many of his ideas are still used today.

In Philadelphia, Franklin started a group called Junto. The group wanted to improve the city. So they created a lending library. They put all the books they owned in the library.

Junto sold library memberships to people. Library members could borrow books. This was a new and exciting idea. Today, libraries are found all over the country.

Franklin owned a newspaper. He shared his ideas in it. He published articles about fire safety. In his day, fires were common. People used fireplaces to provide heat. They used candles for light. Most buildings were made of wood, so fires spread rapidly.

People read Franklin's articles about the dangers of fires. They worried about fire safety. So Franklin created the first volunteer fire department. People were excited to help. Philadelphia became famous for its fire safety, which was the best in the world.

Later Franklin was made the Philadelphia postmaster. He invented a machine to improve mail delivery. He called it an odometer. Franklin attached the odometer to a carriage. This helped figure out the fastest delivery routes. Franklin's efficient system helped deliver mail in half the time. It became the model for the modern United States Postal Service.

In Franklin's day, there were no hospitals. Luckily, Franklin still had more ideas! He got permission from the government to build a public hospital. He helped raise money to build one. In 1751, the first hospital in the American colonies was built.

Name: _____

Benjamin Franklin was always thinking of ways to make life better. He was an author, a printer, a publisher, a musician, an inventor, a scientist, a statesman, and a diplomat. He believed everyone should be a good citizen. He also believed that by working together for the common good, people could accomplish great things.

Accuracy: # of reading errors: _____ (Indep. = 0–6, Instr. = 7–16, Frust. = 17+)
Speed: To calculate: 19440 ÷ _____ (Reading time in seconds) = _____ WPM

 ImagineLearning·

Leveled Books: Ben's Big Ideas

Ben's Big Ideas

Lesson 68
Paired with *The Can Dance*

Discover Story Vocabulary	colonial, community, good citizen
Glossary Words	memberships, governments, good citizen

Question Type	Question
Effect	What was one effect of Franklin publishing articles about fire safety? a. People tried to make Philadelphia safe from fires. b. There were no more fires in cities. c. People stopped using candles in their homes.
Vocabulary	Read this sentence from the article: "The government built a <u>public</u> hospital." What does "public" mean? a. very large b. open to everyone c. only for people who have government jobs
Setting	Where did this article take place? a. New York City b. Boston c. Philadelphia

Name: _____

Main Idea and Supporting Detail: Ben's Big Ideas

* Directions: Fill in the empty boxes with some of Ben's ideas, and then write a summary of the article.

Start a library

Ben's big ideas

My summary of the article

Graphic Organizer: Ben's Big Ideas
Copyright © Imagine Learning, Inc.

115

Name: _____

Weightless in Space

Lesson 69

Paired with *Sir Isaac Newton*

Written by Raymond Lamborn
Illustrated by Maryn Roos

Lexile®: 670L, 114 words

Did you know that your weight would be different in space?

You'd weigh much less on Mars, but you'd weigh lots more on Jupiter.

How does your weight change? It's all about gravity. Any two bodies in space pull towards each other. That pull is called gravity.

Earth is much bigger than you, so it pulls you tightly to its surface. That pull is what a scale measures.

On a small planet, the pull would be less, so you would weigh less. On a big planet, the pull would be much stronger, so you would weigh more.

If you'd like to learn more about gravity and space, you might want to become an astronaut!

| Accuracy: # of reading errors: _____ (Indep. = 0–2, Instr. = 3–6, Frust. = 7+) |
| Speed: To calculate: 6840 ÷ _____ (Reading time in seconds) = _____ WPM |

Leveled Books: Weightless in Space
Copyright © Imagine Learning, Inc.

Name: _____

Weightless in Space

Lesson 69
Paired with *Sir Isaac Newton*

Discover Story Vocabulary	weight, gravity
Glossary Words	weight, planet, gravity, surface, weigh

Question Type	Question
Compare	If you were on a smaller planet than earth, you would weigh _____. a. more b. the same c. less
Inferential	If a spaceship got close to a large planet, gravity would _____. a. send the spaceship out in space b. keep the spaceship away from the planet c. pull the space ship toward the planet
Author's Purpose	Why did the author probably write this article? a. to help people understand astronauts b. to teach people about gravity c. to teach people how to lose weight

Response Journal

Think about the article **Weightless in Space**.

This is a science article. Write about your favorite subject in school. Why do you like it? What kinds of things do you learn?

OR

Does this article make you think about something you've read, heard, or seen? Write about it.

_____

_____

_____

_____

_____

_____

_____

_____

_____

_____

WORDS YOU MIGHT USE

science	math	reading
writing	social studies	geography
PE	art	music

Name: _____

Sir Isaac Newton

Lesson 70

Paired with *Weightless in Space*

Written by Raymond Lamborn
Illustrated by Jim Madsen

Lexile®: 550L, 114 words

Isaac Newton loved math and science.

He was very smart, but he wasn't a star student in school. He learned best when he was by himself.

After two years in college, Isaac got the chance to study on his own because his school closed. A terrible disease made it unsafe for students to go to school.

In the two years Isaac was out of school, he discovered many important ideas. He created a new kind of math.

He discovered gravity. He learned how the sun and planets move.

When he went back to school, his ideas amazed his teachers.

He became a very famous scientist. And his ideas are still important to science today.

Accuracy: # of reading errors: _____ (Indep. = 0–2, Instr. = 3–6, Frust. = 7+)

Speed: To calculate: 9840 ÷ _____ (Reading time in seconds) = _____ WPM

Sir Isaac Newton

Lesson 70
Paired with *Weightless in Space*

Discover Story Vocabulary	discover, disease, scientist
Glossary Words	disease, discovered, scientist

Question Type	Question
Main Idea	What was this article mainly about? a. Isaac Newton's life b. Isaac Newton's school c. Isaac Newton's family
Inferential	Why is Sir Isaac Newton so famous? a. He figured out how to become a good student. b. His discoveries are important to science. c. He didn't get a terrible disease.
Solution	When Newton's college had to close, what did Newton do to get educated? a. He went to a different college. b. He took classes from a famous scientist. c. He studied on his own.

Main Idea and Supporting Detail: Sir Isaac Newton

✱ **Directions:** Fill in the empty boxes, and then write a summary of the article.

Newton's Discoveries

gravity

My summary of the article

Graphic Organizer: Sir Isaac Newton

Name: _____

Museums

Lesson 71
Paired with *Symbols and Secrets—Advanced*

Written by Anna Matola
Illustrated by Maryn Roos
Lexile®: 670L, 210 words

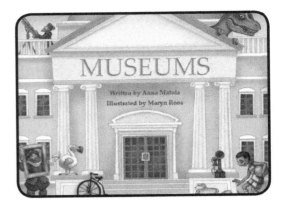

Where do you find mummies and monsters, dinosaurs and diamonds? Not under your bed, not in a cave, and not at the school playground. You can see all four in one place: a museum!

Museums are built to protect important things that teach us about the world. You can visit museums of art and museums of history. There are museums of sports and museums of money.

Kids usually like museums that let them touch and play with things. Check out this insect museum! This girl is holding a live tarantula, and she seems to be having a good time!

Sometimes museums display items that are rare or unusual. For example, take a look at this gigantic beetle. And look at this skeleton of a two-headed snake. Only one in 10,000 snakes is born with two heads, so you'll probably never see one in real life!

Some museums show things from the past, such as this old clock and this old desk.

And some museums have paintings and statues. Aren't these statues amazing? They represent the armies of the first emperor of China, and they were made over two thousand years ago.

Museums are great places to visit. You can have fun and learn a lot at the same time.

| Accuracy: # of reading errors: _____ (Indep. = 0–5, Instr. = 6–11, Frust. = 12+) |
| Speed: To calculate: 12600 ÷ _____ (Reading time in seconds) = _____ WPM |

Imagine Learning®

Name: _____

Museums

Lesson 71
Paired with *Symbols and Secrets—Advanced*

| Discover Story Vocabulary | display, unusual |
| Glossary Words | usually, display, amazing |

Question Type	Question
Main Idea	The main idea of this article is _____. a. people should not touch things in museums b. there are many kinds of interesting museums c. museums are unusual and hard to find
Vocabulary	In this article, the phrase "check out" means _____. a. take away b. look at c. mark this
Literal	Some museums _____. a. let kids touch things b. let kids keep the displays c. let kids bring their pets in to visit

Response Journal

Think about the article **Museums**.

Write about a time where you went to a museum or a place like a museum. Where was it? What did you see? How did you like it?

OR

Think of what kind of museum you would like to visit? Explain why you would want to go there? Why do you think museums are important?

_____

_____

_____

_____

_____

_____

_____

_____

_____

_____

WORDS YOU MIGHT USE

I remember when...	paintings	display
If I could visit...	collection	explore
unusual	interesting	statues
important		

Response Journal: Museums (Advanced)
Copyright © Imagine Learning, Inc.

Name: _____

Symbols and Secrets

Lesson 72

Paired with *Museums—Advanced*

Written by Anna Matola
Illustrated by Nate Baertsch

Lexile®: 700L, 475 words

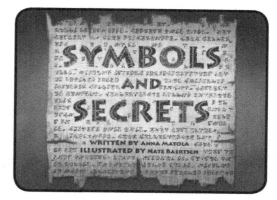

"And this symbol often stood for hidden treasure," said the museum guide, pointing to a framed picture of a rock. Unusual shapes were scratched on its surface.

"I think I've seen something like that at my grandpa's house," whispered Mike to Kayla.

"Now wait a minute—what are the chances of that?" asked Kayla, looking at him in disbelief.

"C'mon, I'll show you," Mike insisted as they hurried from the museum.

They arrived at Grandpa's house, ten minutes later, out of breath. "Grandpa," Mike said excitedly, "we think your house has a hidden treasure!"

Surprised, Grandpa asked, "Now, son, I've been living in this house for more than thiry years. If there's a treasure here, don't you think I would have found it by now?"

"No, because it's a *hidden* treasure," said Mike, emphasizing the word *hidden*. "And I think I know how to find it! So—can we look for it, please?" Mike pleaded.

They looked in every room in the house, but there was no symbol and no hidden treasure. Kayla looked doubtfully at Mike, who was scratching his head. "Are you certain you saw something in this house?" Kayla asked Mike.

"Let's try the attic," suggested Grandpa, looking at their disappointed faces.

They looked in every corner of the attic. Again there was no symbol and no hidden treasure.

"I'm tired," groaned Mike as he headed toward the stairs. "Maybe I was wrong about that symbol. Why would there be a hidden treasure in your house, anyway?"

Name: _____

"Wait!" said Kayla, as she pointed at the chimney, her mouth wide open. "Look at that brick at the bottom of the chimney! Isn't that the symbol we're looking for? Maybe the treasure is hidden in the chimney!"

Mike rushed over to the brick and pulled on it. He gasped in surprise as the brick moved a little. Suddenly, part of the wall slid open, showing the top of a staircase.

"Wow," whispered Mike as they peered into the dark passage. He looked sideways at Kayla and asked excitedly, "Now do you believe me? I hope the treasure is still down there!" He stared at the dark passage, nervously.

"There's only one way to find out!" said Kayla, and she bounded down the staircase.

"Hey! Look over here!" shouted Kayla, dusting the cobwebs off an antique box. "I think we found it!"

Mike and Kayla's discovery made history!

When Mike and Kayla returned the jewel to the museum, they were treated like heroes!

"We have been searching for this jewel for a long time," said the museum guide. "Thank you so very much for returning it."

"No problem," said Mike.

"And to show our appreciation, we'd like to give all of you lifetime passes to the museum."

Grandpa smiled, looking down at his pass. "I wonder what new adventures we'll have together!"

Accuracy: # of reading errors: _____	(Indep. = 0–10, Instr. = 11–24, Frust. = 25+)
Speed: To calculate: 28500 ÷ _____	(Reading time in seconds) = _____ WPM

Symbols and Secrets

Lesson 72
Paired with *Museums—Advanced*

Discover Story Vocabulary	symbol, guide, nervously
Glossary Words	guide, treasure, attic, symbol, passage, nervously, discovery

Question Type	Question
Cause	What caused the wall in the attic to slide open? a. Grandpa opened the door to the staircase. b. Mike pulled on the brick that showed a symbol. c. Kayla pushed on the symbol on the chimney.
Contrast	How is Mike different from Kayla? a. Mike is nervous and Kayla is not afraid. b. Mike is brave and Kayla is worried. c. Mike wants to keep looking and Kayla wants to quit.
Plot	What happened just after Mike and Kayla left the museum? a. They found the treasure. b. They went up to the attic. c. They went to Mike's grandpa's house.

Name: _____

Story Map: Symbols and Secrets

✻ Directions: Fill in the empty boxes, and then write a summary of the story.

Characters:

Setting:

Problem:
Mike and Kayla are trying to find the symbol for hidden treasure.

Plot:

Solution:

My Summary of the story

Graphic Organizer: Symbols and Secrets (Advanced)
Copyright © Imagine Learning, Inc.

✕ ImagineLearning®

Name: _____

Curtains Up

Lesson 73

Paired with *The Case of Missing Manny*

Written by Lisa Salazar and Alex
Illustrated by Maryn Roos

Lexile®: 630L, 537 words

I've always wanted to be a famous author, so, not long ago, I wrote a story.

Maybe you read it. It's called First Place. Now, with a little bit of help, I wrote a play too! Since I know all the tricks, I can teach you how it's done.

If you have ever written a story, you already know the basic steps to writing a play. You first have to decide three different things: the setting, characters, and plot. Each is important, and each one affects the other.

The setting describes when and where the play takes place. This is an important decision because it will change the way your characters interact. Think of how different your play would be if you set it in a scary castle, or in the jungle, or even on the moon! The time period and place can help you decide what your characters wear and how they act.

Now you have to create your characters. You not only have to choose their names but you have to answer other questions, too: How old are they? What do they like to do? What are they afraid of? What is their family like? What do they look like? The more answers you can come up with, the more real your character will become.

The plot describes what will happen to these characters. In the beginning, they have a problem that needs to be solved. The main characters spend most of the play trying to solve the problem.

If you have a hard time creating the plot, use the setting and characters you made up to help you figure it out. For example, if you decided the setting is on the moon, the problem could be that the spaceship broke down. Or, if you decided the main character is afraid of the dark, the plot could be about the night the electricity went out.

Now you have made all the important decisions. You know what's going to happen. You know who it's going to happen to. You know when and where it will happen. Looks like you are ready to start writing the script. This is where writing a play becomes very different from writing a story.

Name: _____

In a story, you write in sections, or chapters. A play is written by scene. Every time the characters go to a different place, a new scene begins. Stage directions explain where the characters are and what the characters do while they talk. These directions are written in italics, so you don't get confused.

The first time you read a play, read the parts in italics out loud. Then you'll know what each character should be doing.

A play is written in dialogue. Each character has lines to memorize that are in the script. When a new character is supposed to speak, that character's name is written in capital letters. This makes the name stand out, but it is not read out loud.

Now that you know how a script is written, you're ready to read my play! It's called The Case of Missing Manny. It all happens on a movie set, and it's full of movie stars and clues. Get ready for lights, camera, and action!

| Accuracy: # of reading errors: _____ (Indep. = 0–11, Instr. = 12–27, Frust. = 28+) |
| Speed: To calculate: 32220 ÷ _____ (Reading time in seconds) = _____ WPM |

Name: _____

Curtains Up

Lesson 73
Paired with *The Case of Missing Manny*

Discover Story Vocabulary	main character, script
Glossary Words	main characters; script; dialogue; lights, camera, and action

Question Type	Question
Literal	What three things do you have to decide before you write a play? a. the setting, characters, and plot b. the author, publisher, and main idea c. the chapters, the number of words, and the capitalization
Vocabulary	The setting of a play is _____. a. where a play happens b. who the people are in a play c. what happens during the play
Author's Purpose	Why did the author write this article? a. to show what is in chapters in stories b. to tell how actors are picked for plays c. to explain how to write a play

Name: _____

Response Journal

Think about the article **Curtains Up**.

Write about the time you saw a play. Where did you see it? How was it different from seeing a movie? Did you like it? What is your opinion of seeing a play?

OR

Write about your favorite story or movie. Describe the setting. Describe two of the characters. Summarize what happened in the story or movie.

_____

_____

_____

_____

_____

_____

_____

_____

_____

WORDS YOU MIGHT USE

actors	dialogue	music
scenery	audience	program
curtains	special effects	characters
similar	different	

Name: _____

The Case of Missing Manny

Lesson 74

Paired with *Curtains Up*

Written by Lisa Salazar and Alex
Illustrated by Maryn Roos

Lexile®: n/a, 712 words

Classroom Activities

Cast of Characters

Detective Ace, *a smart detective*

Carmen Starr, *a beautiful actress*

Bob, *a stylish costumer*

Bonnie, *a sneezing supporting actress*

Barney, *a grumpy cameraman*

Scene 1: Detective Ace's office. He is working on the Case of the Bottle Bandit, someone who steals bottles of expensive perfume. The phone rings.

ACE: Hello?

VOICE: Ace! Ace! Come quick! He's gone!

ACE: Who's gone? Come where?

VOICE: To the movie set. Manny's missing!

Scene 2: The set of a pirate movie. Detective Ace enters.

CARMEN: I'm so glad you're here. It's just terrible. My own costar—missing! Maybe I'll be next.

ACE: So Manny is your costar. Can you describe him for me, Miss—?

CARMEN: Carmen. Carmen Starr. Well, he has nice green eyes, a loud voice, and stands about 2 feet tall.

Ace looks surprised.

CARMEN: Oh, I didn't tell you? He's a parrot.

CARMEN: He was taken last night. The good news is the movie camera was left on by mistake, so we caught his kidnapper on tape.

ACE: So who did it?

CARMEN: That's the bad news. The camera ran out when Manny was naming his kidnapper!

Carmen plays the film, and we see Manny say, "I should have known it would be you, Bah--!"

ACE: Bah, huh? Get me a list of everybody on the set whose name begins with the sound "bah." We'll find that bird bandit!

Scene 3: Costume shop. There are costume pieces everywhere. Ace interviews Bob.

ACE: So, Bob, you made all the costumes for this movie, right?

BOB: Yeah. Another pirate movie. Big deal.

Ace raises his eyebrows.

BOB: Don't get me wrong. I love Manny. But I hate pirate movies! I'd do anything to make some cool alien costumes!

Scene 4: Bonnie's dressing room. Bonnie, the supporting actress, is allergic to everything.

BONNIE: I didn't do it! Manny and I were almost costars! Until I found out I was... ACHOO!

ACE: Allergic to feathers? Seems like a good reason to get rid of a parrot.

BONNIE: But it couldn't have been me. I was on vacation all week. I just got back today!

Scene 5: Backstage. Ace interviews Barney, the short, stubby cameraman.

ACE: So, Barney. Have you always wanted to be a cameraman?

BARNEY: No way! I wanted to be the director, but they hired me as a cameraman instead. They were headed for trouble.

ACE: So for revenge you got rid of the main character?

BARNEY: Hey! That ain't fair. It wasn't me. Besides, why would I have left the camera on if I was planning to steal the bird? It just don't make sense.

Just then, Carmen walks by. Both men nearly fall over.

BARNEY: *calling out behind her,* **Nice perfume, Miss Starr.**

Ace laughs, and then stops. He thinks for a minute and then...

ACE: That's it! I know who did it! Barney, gather everybody together and meet me back here in five minutes!

Scene 6: Backstage, five minutes later. Bob, Bonnie, and Barney are nervous. Carmen is excited.

CARMEN: So, Ace! Did you figure out which one of these crooks took Manny?

ACE: Yes. It wasn't Bob. Or Bonnie. Or Barney. No, someone else had an even better reason to keep Manny quiet.

The three suspects are relieved. Carmen is confused.

CARMEN: Well, then who took Manny?

ACE: You did, Miss Starr. Or should we call you … the Bottle Bandit?

Bob, Bonnie, and Barney gasp.

BONNIE: She's the Bottle Bandit? The one who keeps stealing expensive per-per-per-CHOO! Perfumes?

Carmen tries to escape, but they catch her first.

CARMEN: Let go! You can't do this to me!

ACE: I found this article about the Bottle Bandit under Manny's cage. He discovered her identity, so Carmen had to get rid of him before he told the police.

CARMEN: You have no proof!

ACE: No?

Ace empties out Carmen's purse, and perfume bottles and parrot feathers fall out.

ACE: Manny wasn't saying Bob, Bonnie, or Barney. He was calling you the "Bottle Bandit."

BARNEY: So, Bottle Bandit, where's the bird?

CARMEN: *defeated,* **At the city zoo. I told them he went crazy, so they'd ignore everything he said. They were happy to get a talking parrot. I was happy to put him behind bars.**

ACE: And now, you'll be the only one behind bars. Now that we know where to find Manny, the Case of the Missing Manny—and the Bottle Bandit—is closed.

Accuracy: # of reading errors: _____ (Indep. = 0–14, Instr. = 15–36, Frust. = 37+)
Speed: To calculate: 42720 ÷ _____ (Reading time in seconds) = _____ WPM

Name: _____

The Case of Missing Manny

Lesson 74 (nonstandard prose: play)
Paired with *Curtains Up*

Discover Story Vocabulary	perfume, scene, mystery
Glossary Words	bandit, perfume, scene, suspects, expensive

Question Type	Question
Inferential	Why does Ace suspect Bob, Barney, and Bonnie of taking Manny? a. They each needed the money they could get from selling Manny. b. They each had a reason to want Manny gone. c. They each had read the article about the Bottle Bandit.
Intertextual	When you read the play *The Case of Missing Manny*, what shows you that a character is speaking? a. capital letters b. bolded letters c. lowercase letters
Inferential	What clues did Ace find in Carmen's purse? a. a newspaper article about the Bottle Bandit b. feathers and perfume bottles c. bird seed and a zoo ticket

Name: _____

Story Map: The Case of Missing Manny

✱ Directions: Fill in the empty boxes, and then write a summary of the story.

Characters:

Setting:

Problem:
Detective Ace needs to find out who might have taken Manny, a parrot in a movie.

Plot:

Solution:

My Summary of the story

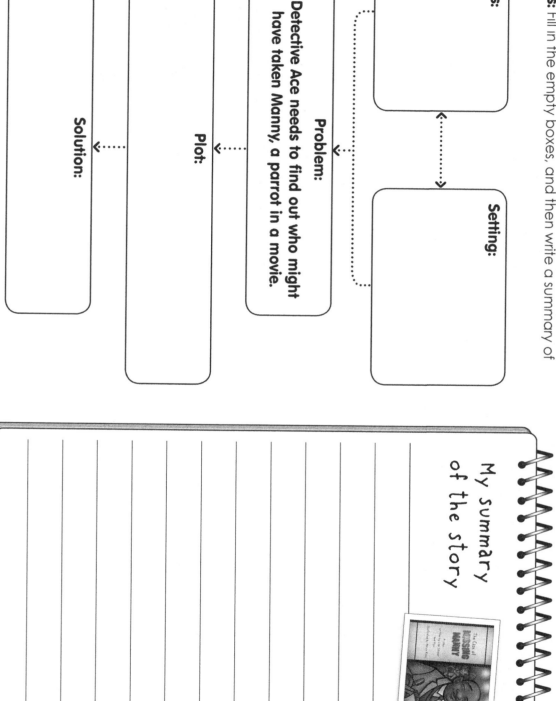

Graphic Organizer: The Case of Missing Manny

Name: _____

Classroom Activities

Hide and Seek

Lesson 75

Paired with *Petroglyphs—Advanced*

Written by Rebecca Suares
Illustrated by Jim Madsen

Lexile®: 650L, 271 words

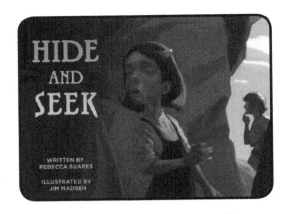

I was scooting on my belly under the brush, so Josh wouldn't see me. If I could reach the car before Josh found me, I'd win the game.

Josh was just a few feet away from me, and I could hear his footsteps heading straight for me. If I made any noise at all, he'd find me, and I'd be out of the game.

"I can hear you, Sandy. I'm going to find you," I heard Josh holler.

As I snaked toward the car, I made a wrong turn and was blocked by a solid wall of rock.

Quickly, I slid along the wall, looking for a way around it.

Off to my left, I could barely make out a dark line on the rock. I inched over to it, hoping it was a crack I could hide in. Josh would never find me there.

I'd wait for him to pass, and then I'd dash for the car before he could find me. I slithered over to the line.

Sure enough, it was a narrow crack in the rock. I planned to hide for a few seconds until Josh passed by, but then I saw something.

Wow! That was no simple crack in the rock. It was a secret entrance to an ancient room!

The rock walls were covered with strange drawings. I forgot all about the game and yelled "Hey, Josh! Come over here. Look what I found! This is so cool!"

"Awesome!" he gasped, as he squeezed through the crack. "They're petroglyphs, Sandy. Let's show Mom and Dad. Oh, and by the way—you're out. I win the game."

Accuracy: # of reading errors: _____	(Indep. = 0–5, Instr. = 6–14, Frust. = 15+)
Speed: To calculate: 16260 ÷ _____	(Reading time in seconds) = _____ WPM

Name: _____

Hide and Seek

Lesson 75
Paired with *Petroglyphs—Advanced*

Discover Story Vocabulary	hide and seek, entrance, ancient
Glossary Words	holler, narrow, ancient, you're out

Question Type	Question
Inferential	Why does Josh probably think the petroglyphs are so amazing? a. They were made by ancient people. b. They are in the desert. c. They are worth a lot of money.
Solution	What was Sandy's problem as she tried to get to the car? a. A rock wall blocked her way. b. She got stuck in the rock wall. c. Josh found her hiding.
Character	Who were the main characters in this story? a. the ancient people b. Josh's parents c. Josh and Sandy

Response Journal

Think about the story **Hide and Seek**.

Write about games you play with your friends. When and where do you play? Who do you play with?

OR

Does this story make you think about something in your own life? Does it make you think of something you've read or seen? Write about it.

_____

_____

_____

_____

_____

_____

_____

_____

_____

_____

WORDS YOU MIGHT USE

This story reminds me of...	score	celebration
rules	equipment	exciting
competition		

Response Journal: Hide and Seek (Advanced)
Copyright © Imagine Learning, Inc.

Name: _____

Petroglyphs

Lesson 76

Paired with *Hide and Seek—Advanced*

Written by Marnae Wilson
Illustrated by Jim Madsen
Lexile®: 650L, 137 words

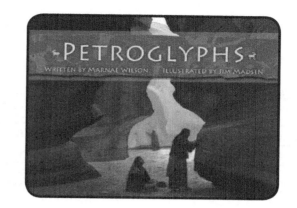

Suppose you have a great story to write, but you have no paper or pencil. How would you save your story?

Thousands of years ago, people scratched pictures on rock to tell their history.

They would show what they did every day. They would draw pictures of their families and their favorite animals.

They would draw pictures to tell stories about their adventures and the places that they had visited.

Petroglyphs are found all over the world.

Some are clear and easy to see. Others have almost disappeared because the weather has caused the rocks to erode.

Sometimes people damage petroglyphs by touching them or writing on them.

Sometimes petroglyphs are destroyed when roads or buildings are built.

We need to be sure petroglyphs are protected. They tell us the history of people who lived long ago.

Accuracy: # of reading errors: _____ (Indep. = 0–3, Instr. = 4–7, Frust. = 8+)
Speed: To calculate: 8220 ÷ _____ (Reading time in seconds) = _____ WPM

Name: _____

Petroglyphs

Lesson 76
Paired with *Hide and Seek—Advanced*

Discover Story Vocabulary	petroglyph, history
Glossary Words	history, petroglyphs, erode, damage, protected

Question Type	Question
Author's Purpose	Why did the author write this article? a. to explain how people make petroglyphs today b. to show how important petroglyphs are c. to tell us how to write our histories
Compare	**Writing Stories** | Today	Long Ago
	petroglyphs | What belongs in the empty box above? a. cameras b. books c. rocks
Inferential	What are some things that would be included in a person's history? a. where and how they lived b. names of the muscles in their body c. kinds of fish in the ocean

Name: _____

Main Idea and Supporting Detail:

✳ Directions: Fill in the empty boxes with information about petroglyphs. Then write a summary of the article.

Petroglyphs

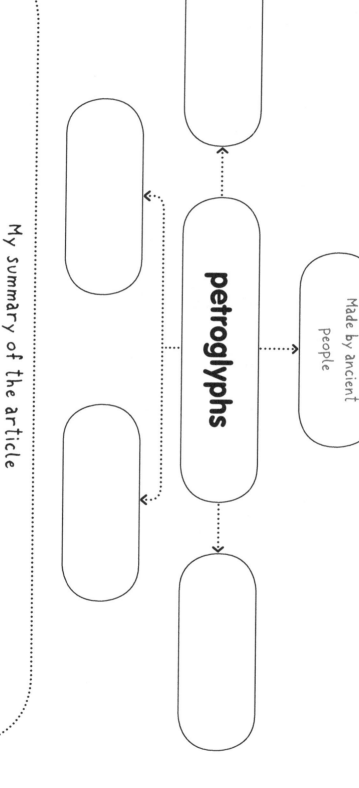

petroglyphs

Made by ancient people

My summary of the article

Graphic Organizer: Petroglpyhs (Advanced)

Name: _____

A Party Surprise

Lesson 77

Paired with *World of Celebrations—Advanced*

Written by Marnae Wilson
Illustrated by Jim Madsen

Lexile®: 640L, 376 words

Whack! The swinging piñata is hit hard, and everyone laughs and cheers. A piñata is a hollow shape that is filled with candy. When someone breaks it open, everyone gets a treat.

You can make your own piñata. You must first get some paper and a balloon. Newspaper is best, because it is inexpensive and easy to use. Then decide what balloon to use. Now you're ready to begin.

First, make a paste by mixing flour and water. Stir the paste until it becomes thick and smooth. Then blow up the balloon. Next, tear the paper into short strips. Finally, dip each strip into the paste and lay it on the balloon. Smooth it down with your hands to remove any bumps. Cover the whole balloon with the paper strips, but make sure you leave an opening at the top.

Now let the paper get very dry. When the paper feels hard, pop the balloon. Surprise! You have an empty ball.

It's time to decorate the empty ball. You can use ribbons, paper, or feathers. You can glue on anything that is bright and colorful. Be creative and decorate it any way you want.

Now fill your piñata with candy, treats, or small gifts. Small, hard candy that is wrapped works best because it doesn't break easily when the piñata is hit. And when it lands on the ground, it won't get dirty. Make sure there is enough candy for everyone to get a piece.

Your piñata is finally ready. Now it's time for a party! Hang your piñata from a tree. Cover someone's eyes with a cloth, and then let them try to hit the piñata with a stick. One hit probably won't break the piñata, so let people take turns swinging the stick.

Finally the piñata will split open. Everyone will cheer and grab for the treats that spill to the ground. Some kids will quickly fill both hands with candy, while

Name: _____

others might only get a piece or two. But everyone will have fun scrambling for treats.

Piñatas are fun to make and break. They have been popular in Mexico for a long time. But Mexico isn't the only country that plays with piñatas. They are fun for parties all over the world.

Accuracy: # of reading errors: _____ (Indep. = 0–8, Instr. = 9–19, Frust. = 20+)
Speed: To calculate: 22560 ÷ _____ (Reading time in seconds) = _____ WPM

Name: _____

A Party Surprise

Lesson 77
Paired with *World of Celebrations—Advanced*

Discover Story Vocabulary	piñata, Mexico
Glossary Words	piñata, hollow, inexpensive, probably

Question Type	Question

Cause

Cause		Effect
	→	The piñata breaks open.

Choose the best answer to go in the empty box.

a. Hit the piñata with a balloon as hard as you can.
b. Hit the piñata hard with a stick.
c. Drop the piñata on the ground so hard that it breaks.

Author's Purpose

What is the main reason the author wrote this article?

a. to describe how to decorate a piñata
b. to describe parties in Mexico
c. to explain how to make a piñata

Literal

After you pop the balloon, what should you do next?

a. decorate the empty ball
b. cover the paper with paste
c. wait for the paper to get dry

Name: _____

Response Journal

Think about the article **A Party Surprise**.

Write about your favorite party or plan a fun party. Include details about the decorations, games, and food.

OR

Write about something that you have made (like a cake, a school project, or a kite). How did you make it? Explain each step you took to make the item.

_____

_____

_____

_____

_____

_____

_____

_____

_____

_____

WORDS YOU MIGHT USE

hilarious	delicious	before
entertaining	first	during
exciting	second	after

Name: _____

World of Celebrations

Lesson 78

Paired with *A Party Surprise—Advanced*

Written by Marnae Wilson
Illustrated by Jim Madsen

Lexile®: 680L, 550 words

All over the world, people get together to celebrate. They celebrate birthdays, religious holidays, and national holidays. And each culture celebrates in a different way. Some people make special holiday foods. Some wear special holiday clothes. Some have special holiday parties. Here's a look at a few celebrations around the world.

Kauai is one of the Hawaiian Islands in the Pacific Ocean.

In Kauai, people have had fun at the Coconut Festival for many years. Coconuts grow at the top of tall, thin palm trees. Every part of the coconut tree is useful. The trunk can be used for wood, and the leaves can be used to make mats and roofs. The nut can be eaten or pressed to get oil. The husk and shell can be burned for fuel.

During the festival, Hawaiians have coconut contests. Who can be the first one to the top of a coconut palm? Who can crack a coconut open the fastest? Who can make the best food using coconuts? Kids paint the coconuts, and teenagers play ball with them. Men and women make clothes out of their leaves. And performers dance and sing. Coconuts are very important to Hawaiians, so at the Coconut Festival, people celebrate coconuts.

Just south of Hawaii is the equator. Following the equator east leads to the African continent. The Ivory Coast is located there.

Every year people in the villages make masks. Some of the masks look like animal heads and others look like scary faces. In November, the villagers celebrate the Festival of Masks. They wear their masks and dance while huge drums boom the rhythm. Which dancer moves the most like an animal? Which mask is best? The most skilled dancers in each village get to dance at the national Festival of Masks.

Following the prime meridian north from the Ivory Coast leads to England, part of the European continent.

After a cold winter, the English celebrate the coming of spring on May 1.

Each community has its own party, and they decorate the streets with flowers and greenery. Often, they put up a maypole with wide ribbons hanging from it. Dancers weave the ribbons as they move around the pole. Other groups dance through the streets. Many people wear white clothing. Girls carry flowers and put flowers in their hair. May Day is a time for love and joy.

East of the European continent is the Asian continent. Thailand is at the south end of the Asian continent.

Every April 13, Thai people celebrate the new year with the Water Festival. This festival is a time to honor older relatives. Young people pour water over their grandparents' hands as a sign of respect.

But the Water Festival is mostly for fun. For three days, people play with water. They throw cups of water at people walking by. They shoot water guns at their friends and soak their neighbors with garden hoses. All over the country, people have huge water fights. April is the hottest month of the year in Thailand, and the Water Festival is a fun way to cool down.

Celebrations happen all over the world on all different continents. People eat special meals. They give gifts. And, they have parties. Celebrations are a time to remember traditions and a time to have fun.

Accuracy: # of reading errors: _____ (Indep. = 0–11, Instr. = 12–28, Frust. = 29+)
Speed: To calculate: 33180 ÷ _____ (Reading time in seconds) = _____ WPM

Name: _____

World of Celebrations

Lesson 78
Paired with *A Party Surprise—Advanced*

Discover Story Vocabulary	celebration, continent
Glossary Words	celebrations, continent, relatives, traditions

Question Type	Question
Compare	How are the celebrations in Hawaii and in the Ivory Coast alike? a. People play ball at both celebrations b. People dance at both celebrations. c. People make masks at both celebrations.
Vocabulary	What is an example of a tradition? a. People in Thailand always treat older relatives with respect. b. People in Hawaii live just north of the equator. c. People in the Ivory Coast live in villages.
Author's Purpose	The author would agree that _____. a. Celebrations take a lot of time and money and might not be worth it. b. Celebrations around the world are filled with traditions and fun. c. Celebrations help people to become better dancers.

Name: _____

Main Idea and Supporting Detail:

A World of Celebrations

✱ Directions: Fill in the empty boxes, and then write a summary of the article.

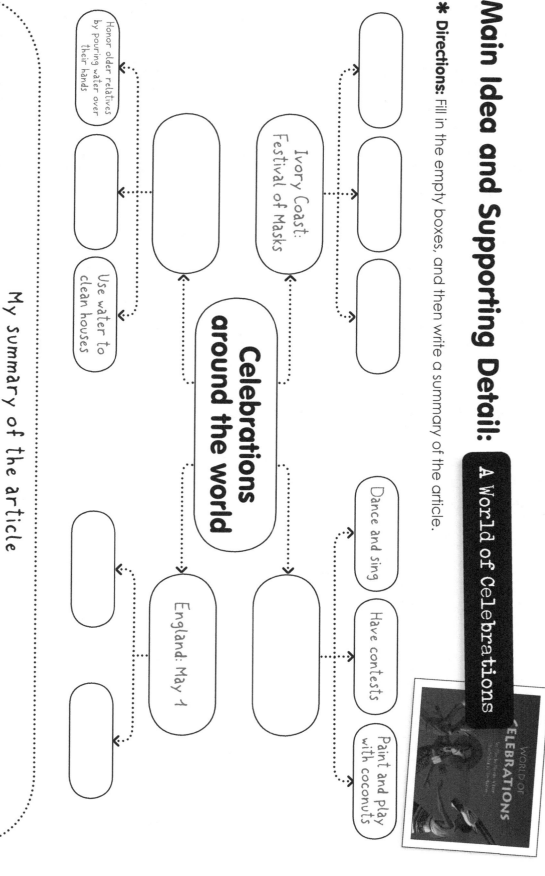

Celebrations around the world

Ivory Coast: Festival of Masks

Honor older relatives by pouring water over their hands

Use water to clean houses

England: May 1

Dance and sing

Have contests

Paint and play with coconuts

My summary of the article

Graphic Organizer: World of Celebrations (Advanced)
Copyright © Imagine Learning, Inc.

151

Name: _____

Rainforest Explorer

Lesson 79

Paired with *Searching*

Written by Nicole Drysdale
Illustrated by Jim Madsen

Lexile®: 760L, 604 words

Congratulations! You've been selected to explore the Amazon Rainforest. Rainforests are the most complex ecosystems on the planet. Because of their wet, warm climates, they support many types of life. The weather, plants, insects, and animals all work together to keep the forest alive.

Rainforests are divided into four layers—we'll spend a day in each! So pack your bags and get ready to explore.

Day 1: The River

One of the best ways to get to the forest is by riding a boat down the Amazon River. This river is the second largest in the world. During the rainy season it floods the forest floor, helping new plants grow. This environment is home to crocodiles, fish, anacondas, and even river dolphins.

Be careful of that caiman hiding in the water. It's the largest crocodile here. The caiman hunts fish and rodents. But it also eats dead animals, helping keep the river clean.

Day 2: The Forest Floor

Floodwaters carry soil from nearby mountains to the forest floor. Nutrients in the soil nourish all the trees and plants. As you can see, this layer is dark and cool. Large animals don't often live in this condition. We'll mostly see insects, frogs, and a few plants.

Do you notice that path of broken leaves? It was left by a colony of leaf-cutter ants. Many leaves fall from the canopy to the forest floor. The ants chop the leaves into chunks and then carry them to their underground nest. This process helps decompose leaves in the forest.

Day 3: The Understory

Today we're moving up into the young trees and shrubs, called the understory. Here it is humid and dark, so the trees grow large leaves in order to capture tiny bits of light. Vines creep around the trees to climb high so they can

reach the light, too. These plants are home to insects, lizards, snakes, and many small creatures.

If you look closely, you may spot a jaguar. Jaguars live on the forest floor and in the understory. Because they are excellent swimmers, runners, and climbers, they are great hunters. They help keep the animals they hunt from overpopulating the forest.

Day 4: The Canopy

Today we're exploring the warmest and brightest layer. In order to get the most light, the trees here grow tall and straight. Branches grow at the top of the trees and spread out to form a roof over the forest. The canopy is the noisiest layer because three-quarters of all Amazon creatures live here, including birds, lizards, and monkeys.

Do you hear the loud chattering? It's a squirrel monkey. These monkeys spend their days searching for fruits, nuts, bird eggs, and insects to munch on. They are messy eaters and often drop bits of their food. This helps feed the animals that live on the forest floor.

Day 5: The Emergent Trees

Let's explore the very top of the forest today. Here the tallest trees thrust themselves above the canopy. It's very windy, but the trees are rewarded with plenty of sunlight. Bird nests, beehives, and a wide variety of flowers and plants are found here.

You may want to get out your binoculars. The bird sitting up there is a sun conure. It is one of the few birds that nest in the emergent trees. Sun conures feed on fruits, berries, and seeds. They often drop seeds, which then grow into new plants.

Day 6: Going Home

This is the end of our grand exploration. The rainforest is one of the most valuable ecosystems because it is home to over half the world's plant and animal species. From the tiny ants to the magnificent jaguar, each organism fills a specific need in the forest. Maybe you can return one day to explore even more.

Accuracy: # of reading errors: _____ (Indep. = 0–14, Instr. = 15–34, Frust. = 35+)
Speed: To calculate: 36240 ÷ _____ (Reading time in seconds) = _____ WPM

 **Imagine Learning®**

Leveled Books: Rainforest Explorer

Rainforest Explorer

Lesson 79
Paired with *Searching*

Discover Story Vocabulary	rainforest, ecosystem, species
Glossary Words	ecosystems, rainforest, nutrients, humid, emergent

Question Type	Question
Effect	**Cause** **Effect** Flooding rivers → Which of the following goes in the empty box? a. force crocodiles to move out of the water b. help new plants grow c. cause trees to lose leaves
Antonym	Read this sentence from the article: "Here it is <u>humid</u> and dark, so the trees grow large leaves in order to capture tiny bits of light." What is an antonym for "humid"? a. dry b. wet c. night
Compare	Squirrel monkeys and sun conures both _____. a. live in the understory of the forest b. drop some of their food onto the forest floor when they eat c. fly above the trees at the top of the forest

Name: _____

Main Idea and Supporting Detail: Rainforest Explorer

✱ Directions: Fill in the empty boxes, and then write a summary of the article.

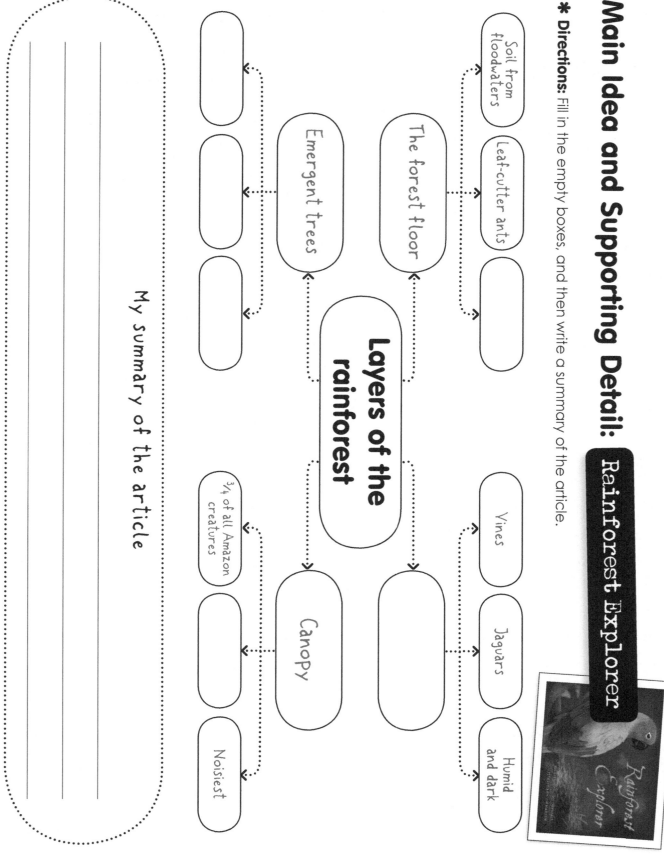

Layers of the rainforest

The forest floor
- Soil from floodwaters
- Leaf-cutter ants
- ( )

Emergent trees
- ( )
- ( )
- ( )

Canopy
- ¾ of all Amazon creatures
- ( )
- Noisiest

( )
- Vines
- Jaguars
- Humid and dark

My summary of the article
_____
_____
_____
_____

Name: _____

Searching

Lesson 80
Paired with *Rainforest Explorer*

Written by Nicole Drysdale
Illustrated by Jim Madsen

Lexile®: n/a, 228 words

Crick, crick, croak. A frog
peeks her head
through the rainforest leaves.
Her eggs are hidden in
the foliage of the floor.

Wiggle, wiggle, squiggle. The eggs
begin to move.
The frog must find a home
where her tadpoles
can grow.

Hop, hop, hop. The frog
starts her search.
She finds a warm, wet stream
where her tadpoles
can grow.

HISS, HISS. A snake
slithers toward the stream
to hunt.
Tadpoles would not be safe
with a snake for a neighbor.

Name: _____

Hop, hop, hop. The frog
moves higher.
She finds a big, thick branch
where her tadpoles
can grow.

GRRR, GROWL. A jaguar
leaps onto the branch
to rest.
Tadpoles would not be cozy
sharing a branch with a jaguar.

Hop, hop, hop. The frog
climbs to the canopy.
She finds a limb's comfy curve
where her tadpoles
can grow.

CHITTER, CHATTER. A monkey
swings to the limb
to eat.
Tadpoles would not be peaceful
with monkeys swinging by.

Hop, hop, hop. The frog
looks around.
She finds a large leafy plant
where her tadpoles
can grow.

Leveled Books: Searching

Name: _____

SPLISH, SPLASH. The frog
plops into a perfect pool of water
to rest.
Tadpoles would be safe, cozy, and peaceful
inside this leafy plant.

Crick, crick, croak. The frog
hops to her hatching eggs.
She carries her tadpoles
up, up, up to the perfect pool
where they will grow
into frogs.

Accuracy: # of reading errors: _____ (Indep. = 0–5, Instr. = 6–11, Frust. = 12+)
Speed: To calculate: 13680 ÷ _____ (Reading time in seconds) = _____ WPM

Leveled Books: Searching
Copyright © Imagine Learning, Inc.

Imagine Learning®

Name: _____

Searching

Lesson 80 (nonstandard prose: poem)
Paired with *Rainforest Explorer*

Discover Story Vocabulary	poetry , onomatopoeia
Glossary Words	foliage, slithers, cozy

Question Type	Question
Problem	What is the problem the mother frog has? a. She needs a place for her babies to grow. b. She needs to keep her eggs dry for them to hatch. c. She needs to find food for her tadpoles.
Intertextual	What animals that live in the canopy are mentioned in "Rainforest Explorer" and "Searching"? a. bees b. monkeys c. lizards
Inferential	Why wouldn't a snake be a good neighbor for tadpoles? a. A snake might eat the tadpoles. b. A snake might push the tadpoles down the stream. c. A snake might make too much noise.

Name: _____

Response Journal

Think about the poem **Searching**.

Rewrite the poem to be a story. Now compare the story and the poem. Which do you like better? Why?

OR

Write a poem about something in nature. Your poem should be at least 6–8 lines. Remember, it doesn't have to rhyme.

_____

_____

_____

_____

_____

_____

_____

_____

_____

_____

WORDS YOU MIGHT USE

tadpoles	foliage	journey
hatch	canopy	travels
peaceful	forest floor	

Response Journal: Searching
Copyright © Imagine Learning, Inc.

Name: _____

The Record Breakers

Lesson 81

Paired with *Picture This*

Written by Lisa Salazar

Illustrated by Jim Madsen

Lexile®: 680L, 540 words

"Whoa! Look at this!" Mario shouted to his friends. "This lady's fingernails are almost as long as I am!"

"Ew, that's gross!" Lena squirmed when she looked at the photo. "That record would take forever to beat, especially for me," Lena said as she looked down at her own bitten fingernails.

"Well, we gotta find some kind of record to break because I want to be famous," Tito declared.

Mario, Lena, and Tito were poring over the Book of World Records looking for a record that they could beat. "Maybe we could earn the world record for holding our breath the longest?" Lena suggested while playing with her gum.

"No good," Mario said. "It says here that someone held his breath for almost ten minutes! We'd never make it."

"We should see who can keep their eyes open the longest," Tito said.

"Sounds easy enough," Mario agreed. "I'll get a stopwatch."

"And I'll make a table," Lena said.

The boys stopped. "A table?" they asked in unison.

"A table will help us to keep track of our times. I'll show you how to make one," Lena explained. "A table has rows and columns. You read rows from side to side, and you read columns from top to bottom. I'll put our names on the top of each column, and then I'll write the record we want to break on the left. And now," Lena put the finishing touches on the table, "we are ready to go!"

And the staring contest began. The three friends stared at each other, but within seconds, Lena failed miserably. Mario blinked soon after, and a minute later, Tito had tears pouring down his face and gave up.

Looking for a different record to break, they decided to try a pretzel eating contest to see who could eat the most pretzels in one minute. Lena forfeited. "I've got gum in my mouth," she protested. Lena always had gum in her mouth. Mario and Tito tried their best, but they got sick after eating only a few handfuls of pretzels.

Next, the three friends tried to see who could sing the same note the longest. They also tried balancing eggs, spoons, and even Thunderclese (Mario's pet goldfish) on their heads. But no one was even close to breaking any records.

"What'll we do now?" Lena was bored with trying to break records, so she was blowing bubbles with her gum to pass the time.

"I know!" Mario said. "Let's see who can blow the biggest bubble!" Mario and Tito chewed on some bubble gum, but they couldn't even blow a bubble as big as their faces.

"My turn!" Lena yelled. Lena chomped on her gum a few more times and then began to blow a bubble. It grew and grew, from two inches to four inches, from six to seven.

"Whoa!" Mario gasped. "She's still going!"

The bubble expanded to ten inches and then eleven.

"It's already twelve inches—that's a whole foot long!" Tito jumped up and down.

And it was only getting bigger. Until...

Pop!

The bubble gum bubble exploded all over Lena's face.

Tito and Mario clapped and shouted. And Lena was still smiling as she filled in the last blank on the table.

| Accuracy: # of reading errors: _____ (Indep. = 0–11, Instr. = 12–27, Frust. = 28+) |
| Speed: To calculate: 32400 ÷ _____ (Reading time in seconds) = _____ WPM |

The Record Breakers

Lesson 81
Paired with *Picture This*

Discover Story Vocabulary	table, break a record
Glossary Words	table, record to break, miserably

Question Type	Question
Literal	In a table, how do you read a column? a. top to bottom b. side to side c. corner to corner
Character	How can you tell Lena is a good organizer? a. She records their information in a table. b. She always has gum in her mouth. c. She gets bored easily.
Synonym	What is a synonym for the word "protested"? a. objected b. agreed c. explained

Name: _____

Problem and Solution: The Record Breakers

✱ Directions: Fill in the empty boxes, and then write a summary of the story.

Problem:

How can they set a new world record?

↓

Possible Solutions:

1. Staring contest
2.
3. Singing the same note the longest
4.

↓

Solution:

Problem:

How can they keep track of each attempt to break a record?

↓

Solution:

They can make a

My summary of the story

_____

_____

_____

_____

Graphic Organizer: The Record Breakers
Copyright © Imagine Learning, Inc.

Ⓧ Imagine Learning®

Name: _____

Picture This

Lesson 82

Paired with *The Record Breakers*

Written by Lisa Salazar
Illustrated by Nate Baertsch

Lexile®: 720L, 531 words

Your teacher asks you to take a survey of which languages the fourth and fifth graders at your school speak—other than English. So you grab a pen and paper and start asking your friends what they speak. You find a few Spanish speakers here, a couple of Vietnamese speakers there. After a couple of hours, and lots of paper, you collect the last bit of data and find yourself with a big mess of numbers and tally marks. Now what?

If only the tally marks meant something. If only there was a clear way to compare the information. If only you could work with pictures and not numbers. Well, picture this. Graphs are a great way to visually organize your information. Start by building a table.

You can put away the hammer and nails. This table has rows and columns, not four legs and a table top. A table allows you to quickly find the information you want. It's a good place to look if you want to find exact data. For example, if you wanted to know how many fifth graders speak Russian, follow the 5th Grade row to the right until you reach the Russian column. Wow—six students in the fifth grade speak Russian!

But what if you wanted to quickly see which language was the most common? There are so many columns that it could take a while to compare the numbers. Picture this. A great way to compare numbers is to make a pie.

But this pie has colors and percentages, not cherries or cream filling. It might not be tasty, but it's very helpful. A pie chart quickly shows how one part compares to the whole. The whole pie represents the total number of students. Each slice represents the number of students that speak a certain language. For example, the Spanish slice is the biggest. That means Spanish is spoken more than all the other foreign languages.

When you looked at the table, it seemed like lots of students speak Vietnamese. Ten students! That's almost half your class. But when you look

 **Imagine Learning**®

at the same information in a pie chart, you see that the Vietnamese slice is very thin. When compared to the 130 students who speak another language, Vietnamese seems much less common.

Now you want to compare the fourth graders to the fifth graders. Which grade has the most Korean speakers? It can be hard to tell which pie slice is bigger. Picture this. You need to use some bars.

But not candy bars! And not metal bars, either. You need a bar graph. Bar graphs are good for quickly comparing lots of information at the same time. The taller the bar is, the higher the number it represents. If you follow the top of the bar to the left, you can see exactly how many students speak each language. Look how easy it is to see that more fourth graders speak Korean than fifth graders do. You can also see that Tagalog is the least common language spoken.

Tables, pie charts, and bar graphs all help to organize data. It all depends on the type of picture you want to see.

Accuracy: # of reading errors: _____ (Indep. = 0–11, Instr. = 12–27, Frust. = 28+)

Speed: To calculate: 31860 ÷ _____ (Reading time in seconds) = _____ WPM

Leveled Books: Picture This

Imagine Learning®

Name: _____

Picture This
Lesson 82
Paired with *The Record Breakers*

| Discover Story Vocabulary | survey, compare, graph |
| Glossary Words | survey, compare, common |

Question Type	Question
Inferential	A pie chart is probably named that because it _____. a. shows information about pies b. is round like a pie c. is so colorful
Literal	Tables show information with rows and _____. a. triangles b. bars c. columns
Main Idea	**Ways of organizing information** pie charts tables [ ] Which of the following goes in the empty box? a. photos b. bars c. bar graphs

Name:_____

Response Journal

Think about the article **Picture This**.

Write about a time you worked on a report for a class. Describe the project. How did you gather information for the report? How did you show the information? Was it successful?

OR

Do you speak another language or do you know someone who does? Give three examples of how speaking two languages can help you.

_____

_____

_____

_____

_____

_____

_____

_____

_____

_____

WORDS YOU MIGHT USE

research	poster	translate
Internet	examples	bilingual
library	difficult	future

Response Journal: Picture This

Name: _____

Davy Crockett: Larger Than Life

Lesson 83

Paired with *Sally Ann Thunder Ann Whirlwind*

Written by Sharlene Petersen
Illustrated by Nate Baertsch

Lexile®: 630L, 378 words

David Crockett was a famous patriot, explorer, and congressman. Stories about his adventures are a mix of facts, opinions, and exaggeration. This kind of story is called a tall tale.

A fact is something that is true. It is a fact that David lived in America. An opinion is a person's belief. It is an opinion that David was a great American hero. Some people may believe that, but others may not.

Here's a look at some of the facts, opinions, and exaggerations about Davy Crockett.

Some say that when Davy was born, he weighed 200 pounds and could jump and dance. Surely he was the strongest, happiest baby in all of Tennessee.

Davy Crockett was born in Tennessee. But unlike the tall tale, he was an average size baby.

When Davy was a young boy, he ran away from home. While walking through the woods, Davy fell into a crack. He wiggled and squirmed, but he couldn't move. He was stuck.

A big bear cub noticed Davy's problem. He thought Davy might be a tasty snack. So he reached down and pulled and tugged until Davy was free.

Davy was so happy he hugged that big bear. And the bear hugged him back! They've been best friends ever since.

The real Davy Crockett did run away from home as a teenager. He worked as a cattle driver and traveled. When he was sixteen, Davy returned home to work and go to school.

Davy married one of the smartest, bravest girls around. Her name was Sally Ann Thunder Ann Whirlwind. They built a nice cabin together.

Name: _____

One night noisy alligators were dancing on the Crockett's roof. Sally Ann and Davy couldn't sleep. So they climbed on the roof and swung those alligators all the way to the Mississippi River.

Davy Crockett did get married and have a family. But his wife's name was not Sally Ann, and they never had alligators on their roof. In both the tall tales and in real life, Davy took care of his family.

Davy loved to tell stories. Most often they were a mix of a few facts, a few opinions, and a lot of exaggeration. Davy Crockett's real adventures and the tall tales about him made him a legendary American hero.

| Accuracy: # of reading errors: _____ (Indep. = 0–8, Instr. = 9–19, Frust. = 20+) |
| Speed: To calculate: 22680 ÷ _____ (Reading time in seconds) = _____ WPM |

Leveled Books: Davy Crockett: Larger Than Life
Copyright © Imagine Learning, Inc.

Name: _____

Davy Crockett: Larger Than Life
Lesson 83
Paired with *Sally Ann Thunder Ann Whirlwind*

| Discover Story Vocabulary | opinion, exaggeration, tall tale |
| Glossary Words | exaggeration, tall tales, noticed, legendary |

Question Type	Question
Author's Purpose	What is the main reason the author wrote this article? a. to prove that tall tales were true b. to teach about tall tales c. to tell about who wrote tall tales
Contrast	The real baby Davy Crockett was _____. a. tiny b. average c. huge
Solution	According to the tall tale, how did a bear solve Davy's problem? a. The bear killed the alligator on Davy's roof. b. The bear showed Davy the way to Tennessee. c. The bear pulled Davy out of a crack.

Name: _____

Compare and Contrast:

Davy Crockett: Larger than Life

* **Directions:** Fill in the empty boxes, and then write a summary of the article.

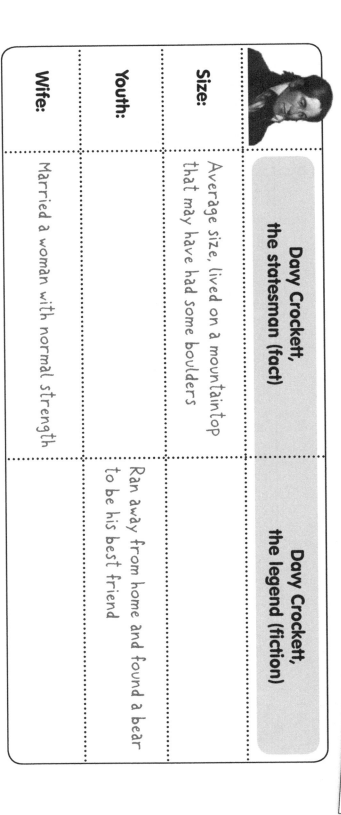

	Davy Crockett, the statesman (fact)	Davy Crockett, the legend (fiction)
Size:	Average size, lived on a mountaintop that may have had some boulders	
Youth:		Ran away from home and found a bear to be his best friend
Wife:	Married a woman with normal strength	

My summary of the article

_____
_____
_____
_____

Graphic Organizer: Davy Crockett: Larger Than Life

Imagine Learning®

Name: _____

Sally Ann Thunder Ann Whirlwind

Lesson 84

Paired with Davy Crockett: Larger Than Life

Written by Sharlene Petersen
Illustrated by Maryn Roos

One hot summer day that was much like every other day, a baby was born who was not much like any other baby. This baby stood up and shouted to the world, "I'm Sally Ann Thunder Ann Whirlwind!" She grinned from ear to ear. "I can outjump, outdance, and outlasso anybody."

Sally Ann's family was amazed. They couldn't help smiling back at the little baby who was a big boaster. They already loved little Sally Ann for all her spunk, but her brothers and sisters didn't believe she could jump higher or dance better or lasso faster than they could. So they challenged her to a jumping contest. They picked the biggest tree in the forest.

"Aww, that's easy," Sally Ann said. "One, two, three, JUMP!"

Ma and Pa, brothers and sisters, and baby Sally Ann all jumped. They tried their best, but only Sally Ann reached the top. They had to admit—she was a pretty talented baby.

Sally Ann grew and so did her love of adventure. So after a few years, she was ready to try things on her own. She grabbed her favorite blanket and said her goodbyes. "I'm heading for the wild," she said. "Wish me some luck."

Knowing the strong gal Sally was, her family said, "We're wishing the wild some luck."

And off she went.

After a long day of hiking, Sally Ann curled up with her blanket for a quick snooze. Suddenly she heard a low growl. Opening her eyes, Sally was face to face with a very large and very angry panther.

"I am so sorry," Sally Ann said. "Have I taken your bed?"

The panther just glared and growled.

"Perhaps we could be friends," she said. "And friends enjoy a good dance.

Name: _____

Would you like to dance with me?"

Now everyone knows that a panther cannot refuse a dance. So that panther stood on his hind legs and danced with Sally Ann. They danced until their feet—and paws—were sore. And they laughed until their sides ached. And when it was all done, they were the best of friends.

Years passed, and Sally Ann grew taller and stronger and braver than ever. One afternoon she heard a loud screeching and went to investigate. What she found made her laugh so loud the trees shook. A man was lying on the ground with his head stuck in the fork of a tree.

"Ouch!" he yelled as he tried to get up.

"How'd you get into this fine mess?" Sally asked.

"I laid down here for a nap and when I woke my head was stuck," the man replied. "Now if you'd be so kind to help a fellow out, I'll give you a nice iron comb," he said.

"Sure as sugar!" Sally Ann said. "But you don't have to give me a comb. I'll help because I like to."

She reached into a snake's den and pulled out a handful of rattlesnakes. Quick as can be, she tied the snakes together to make a mighty strong rope. Then she lassoed that tree and pulled and tugged with all her strength.

The branch bent and the man pulled his head free.

He jumped up to meet his rescuer. The man took one look at Sally Ann and was love-struck.

"I'm Davy Crockett," he said, "and I'd be happier than a huggin' bear if you'd let me call you Mrs. Crockett."

Sally Ann flashed her ear-to-ear grin and said, "I'm Sally Ann Thunder Ann Whirlwind, and I'd be happier than a dancin' panther to be your wife."

So the two got hitched. They built a nice log cabin where they could raise lots of little Crocketts to join in their wild and grand adventures.

Accuracy: # of reading errors: _____ (Indep. = 0–13, Instr. = 14–31, Frust. = 32+)
Speed: To calculate: 37500 ÷ _____ (Reading time in seconds) = _____ WPM

Name: _____

Sally Ann Thunder Ann Whirlwind

Lesson 84

Paired with *Davy Crockett: Larger Than Life*

Discover Story Vocabulary	talented, challenge
Glossary Words	adventure, challenged, lassoed, rescuer, got hitched

Question Type	Question
Synonym	Read this sentence from the story: "So they <u>challenged</u> her to a jumping contest." What is a synonym for the word "challenged"? a. dared b. carried c. introduced
Cause	What caused Sally Ann to leave home? a. She was smarter than her family. b. She wanted more adventures. c. She wanted to get married.
Character	Who were the main characters in this story? a. Sally Ann and Davy Crockett b. Sally Ann and her brothers c. Sally Ann and her dog

Name: _____

Problem and Solution:

✱ Directions: Fill in the empty boxes, and then write a summary of the story.

Sally Ann Thunder Ann Whirlwind

Problem:

Sally wakes up to face
a panther

↓

Solution:

Problem:

↓

Solution:

Sally pulls the tree branch back
using a rattlesnake rope

My summary of the story

_____
_____
_____

Graphic Organizer: Sally Ann Thunder Ann Whirlwind

✖ Imagine Learning®

Name: _____

Board Sports

Lesson 85

Paired with *Inventions*

Written by Sharlene Petersen
Illustrated by Nate Baertsch

Lexile®: 560L, 224 words

Hundreds of years ago, the people of Hawaii created a special board that they used to ride ocean waves.

A rider would begin by lying on the board and paddling toward the waves. He would hold on to the board and dive under most of them.

But when the right wave came, he would stand on the board and ride it to shore. The Hawaiian people had invented the sport of surfing!

Surfers slice through water, hang ten, and get tubed in the waves.

In the 1900's, kids invented a land style of surfing. They attached roller skate wheels to the bottom of wood boards. Then they stood on the board and skated. This sport later became known as skateboarding.

Skateboarders slide on rails. They drop down stairs. They ollie, or jump, over almost anything.

In the 1960's, a man was sledding with his daughter when he thought of a way to surf on snow. He bolted two skis together and attached a rope to the front.

Over many years, different people improved on this design. For example, one person added bindings to the board to attach the rider's feet. This sport is now called snowboarding.

Snowboarders perform many tricks. They jump. They flip. They carve through snow.

Surfing. Skateboarding. Snowboarding. These are some of the extreme sports invented over time.

Accuracy: # of reading errors: _____ (Indep. = 0–4, Instr. = 5–11, Frust. = 12+)

Speed: To calculate: 13440 ÷ _____ (Reading time in seconds) = _____ WPM

Name: _____

Board Sports

Lesson 85
Paired with *Inventions*

Discover Story Vocabulary	invent
Glossary Words	Invented, hang ten, rails

Question Type	Question
Contrast	How is a skateboard different from a snowboard and a surfboard? a. A skateboard can go fast. b. A skateboard has wheels. c. A skateboard has bindings.
Main Idea	What is the best summary of this article? a. Skateboarders slide down rails, drop down stairs, and jump over things. b. People in Hawaii created the sport of surfing. c. People have invented three different boards for sport: the surfboard, the skateboard, and the snowboard.
Plot	Which board sport was invented last? a. snowboarding b. surfing c. skateboarding

Name: _____

Response Journal

Think about the article **Board Sports**.

Write about an extreme sport that you like to watch or you would like to try. Why do you like it? What makes it exciting?

OR

Explain three things you learned about board sports. Include details and examples.

_____

_____

_____

_____

_____

_____

_____

_____

_____

_____

WORDS YOU MIGHT USE

My favorite...	exciting	awesome
tricks	attached	sledding
design	Hawaii	

Response Journal: Board Sports

Name: _____

Inventions

Lesson 86

Paired with Board Sports

Written by Karri Ann Fisher
Illustrated by Nate Baertsch

Lexile®: 650L, 155 words

Sometimes scientists plan inventions. Step by step they figure out how to solve a problem. But sometimes inventions happen without planning. Scientists call this "serendipity."

For example, once a scientist tried to make very strong glue. It didn't work. The glue was very weak. He thought he had failed until he used the glue on little pieces of paper.

That's right—he invented sticky notes.

Another unplanned invention happened when a doctor tried to discover what caused diseases.

He noticed mold growing on some special dishes in his lab. He began to wash the mold away, but then he stopped to take a closer look. He found a chemical that he used to make a medicine called penicillin.

This doctor started out trying to find what caused diseases and ended up finding how to heal diseases. This was a happy accident.

Because of serendipity we have lots of inventions that make our lives better.

Accuracy: # of reading errors: _____ (Indep. = 0–3, Instr. = 4–8, Frust. = 9+)
Speed: To calculate: 9300 ÷ _____ (Reading time in seconds) = _____ WPM

Name: _____

Inventions
Lesson 86
Paired with *Board Sports*

Discover Story Vocabulary	serendipity, medicine, penicillin
Glossary Words	solve, penicillin, unplanned, serendipity

Question Type	Question
Main Idea	What belongs in the empty box? **Inventions** → snowboards, [empty], penicillin, skateboards a. mold b. disease c. sticky notes
Synonym	Read this sentence from the article: "One day this doctor <u>noticed</u> that mold was growing in some Petri dishes." What is a synonym for the word "noticed"? a. observed b. wrote in a notebook c. ignored
Compare	Sticky notes and penicillin were both _____. a. used to treat diseases b. unplanned inventions c. invented by the same doctor

Name: _____

Information Table: Inventions

* **Directions:** Fill in the empty boxes, and then write a summary of the article.

Invention:	How did serendipity lead to this invention?
Velcro	
Sticky notes	Accidentally made "weak" glue
Penicillin	

My summary of the article

_____

_____

Graphic Organizer: Inventions
Copyright © Imagine Learning, Inc.

✗ Imagine Learning®

Name: _____

Your Own Secret Army

Lesson 86

Paired with *Stopping the Killers*

Written by Deborah Taylor
Illustrated by Nate Baertsch

Lexile®: 790L, 197 words

Remember when you got an immunization shot? Did you ever wonder how that shot could stop you from getting sick?

Well, here's how it works. Pretend your body has a secret little army inside that fights diseases. Most of the time this army, called antibodies, just sits around waiting for germs to get into your body.

If germs do get in, the army jumps into action and kills the germs, so you won't get sick.

But sometimes the germs get in and grow so fast that your body's army can't kill them all. Then you get really sick.

So doctors figured out a way to help your body fight diseases. They immunize you. They inject a small number of germs into you to make your army think it's under attack.

Then the army starts making all kinds of weapons and soldiers to kill the germs.

When it figures out that there aren't very many germs to kill, it stores all its weapons and troops.

When a real attack of germs happens, the army is prepared to wipe them out in a hurry. And you don't get sick. You never even notice you've been attacked!

Accuracy: # of reading errors: _____ (Indep. = 0–4, Instr. = 5–10, Frust. = 11+)
Speed: To calculate: 11820 ÷ _____ (Reading time in seconds) = _____ WPM

Name: _____

Your Own Secret Army

Lesson 86
Paired with *Stopping the Killers*

Discover Story Vocabulary	immunize, antibodies
Glossary Words	antibodies, germs, immunize, stores

Question Type	Question
Vocabulary	What is another name for the secret army? a. antibodies b. germs c. shots
Cause	What belongs in the empty box? [empty box] → **Your secret army makes weapons.** a. Antibodies cause disease. b. Germs are destroyed. c. You get an immunization shot.
Effect	What happens when doctors put a few germs in you? a. The army in your body builds up weapons to kill the germs. b. The doctors learn more about germs. c. The germs get stronger and finally make you very sick.

Name: _____

Cause and Effect: Your Own Secret Army

* Directions: Fill in the empty boxes, and then write a summary of the article.

Cause

You get a shot with a few germs

Effect

Cause

You get a real germ attack

Effect

My summary of the article

_____
_____
_____
_____

Graphic Organizer: Your Own Secret Army
Copyright © Imagine Learning, Inc.

Imagine Learning®

Name: _____

Stopping the Killers

Lesson 88

Paired with *Your Own Secret Army*

Written by Deborah Taylor
Illustrated by Jim Madsen

Lexile®: 670L, 234 words

Some diseases, like polio, smallpox, and the flu, are very dangerous. They can pass from one person to another easily. They can even kill people.

Many years ago, doctors began studying these killer diseases. They tried to figure out what made people sick and how to cure them. But they really wanted to stop people from ever getting sick.

These doctors studied the problem. First, they watched people with a disease.

They found out that if the person didn't die from the disease, that person never got the disease again. Next, the doctors tried to guess why people didn't get the same disease twice.

They hypothesized that when people got sick and then got better, their bodies had learned how to kill the germs. Finally, some doctors decided to test this idea. They put a few germs into people's bodies. Then they waited and watched.

There weren't enough germs to make the people sick. Best of all, when these people got near someone with smallpox, they did not get sick! The doctors' idea was right! They had discovered how to keep people from ever getting smallpox.

They tried their idea with other kinds of disease germs, like polio and the measles, and it worked. People didn't get these diseases either.

Now children all over the world get shots to keep them from catching the killer diseases. And the shots protect them all their lives.

Accuracy: # of reading errors: _____ (Indep. = 0–5, Instr. = 6–12, Frust. = 13+)
Speed: To calculate: 10440 ÷ _____ (Reading time in seconds) = _____ WPM

Name: _____

Stopping the Killers

Lesson 88
Paired with *Your Own Secret Army*

Discover Story Vocabulary	observe, hypothesize
Glossary Words	cure, hypothesized, catching

Question Type	Question
Plot	When doctors use the scientific method, they begin by making observations. What do they do next? a. make a hypothesis b. test their idea c. cure people
Inferential	What do doctors put in immunization shots to prevent children from getting sick? a. small pox b. medicine c. a few germs
Intertextual	What is in our bodies that kills germs? (Think of the other article.) a. super strong germs called diseases b. small pox attack cells c. a secret army, called antibodies

Name: _____

Response Journal

Think about the article **Stopping the Killers**.

Write about a time when you had a problem. What was it? How did you solve it?

OR

Write about three things you learned from reading this article.

_____

_____

_____

_____

_____

_____

_____

_____

_____

_____

WORDS YOU MIGHT USE

problem	solved	germs
protect	disease	figure out
for example	difficult	

Response Journal: Stopping the Killers
Copyright © Imagine Learning, Inc.

Notes

Associated Press Articles Guide

Resource Overview

Associated Press (AP) articles are authentic, nonfiction news articles in the grade-level Lexile band. Each article pairs thematically with a related Leveled Book. These relevant and engaging news articles help students learn new vocabulary, improve literacy skills, and increase their knowledge of the world. Article topics include historical, scientific, and technical issues and address real-world problems and questions. Students can analyze the arguments presented, discuss their own opinions, and support arguments using evidence from the text.

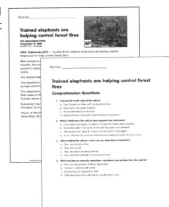

The AP articles and the accompanying Comprehension Questions provide material for whole-class or small-group academic discussions, collaborative research, and individual writing topics. Comprehension Questions focus on helping students learn nonfiction vocabulary and concepts, identify main ideas and supporting details, cite text evidence to support claims, and understand the sequence of events. See the Associated Press Articles Answer Key for the correct answers.

How to Use This Resource in the Classroom

- **Match the Headings:** Select a number of articles and separate the headings from the articles. Display the headings or place them in a central location. Provide students with the articles and ask them to match each one to a headline. Have students point out the words in the headline that helped them to match it to the correct story.

- **Word Hunt:** Have students use the news article to go on a word hunt. Have students work in pairs or teams to hunt for any of the following:
  - Recent vocabulary or spelling words
  - Parts of speech students are learning: adjectives, adverbs, prepositional phrases, etc.
  - New/unknown words (have students look up definitions in the dictionary)

- **Five Words:** Give each student (or pair of students) a different news article. Ask students to choose five interesting words from the article and use them to write original sentences or a short paragraph. Display or write the headlines from the selected articles on the board. Have each student read their original sentences or paragraph. Have the other students in the class listen and use the headlines to try to determine the article that the words came from.

- **KWL Chart:** Use a KWL chart (what I **K**now, what I **W**ant to know, what I have **L**earned) to activate students' prior knowledge of the topic and engage their interest as they read. Before distributing the article, read the headline aloud and ask students what they know about this topic. For example, if the article is about volcanoes, students can write anything they already know about volcanoes in the K column. Have students discuss what they know with a partner or small group. Read the headline again and ask the students what they think they might learn about volcanoes from the article. Then have students write what they want to know about the topic in the W column. Ask them to list two to three items. Choose whether to have students read the text silently, with a partner, or as whole group. After reading, have students write two to three things they learned about the topic in the L column. Have the class summarize and discuss what they learned in the news article.

- **False or Fact:** Have each student read a news article. After reading, have the students decide on two to three facts or details from their article that they want to change. Have students summarize their article to a partner, changing the details as they do. The partner must try to guess which of the facts are true and which facts have been changed.

- **State Connections:** Select any of the United States news articles listed below. Assign students to small groups. Have students read the story and underline names of US states or cities mentioned in the article. Have students begin by locating the state(s) on a map and then ask them to use prior knowledge and classroom resources to answer questions about the state featured in the article, such as: In which US state does the event or story take place? In what area of the United States is the state located? What is the distance between our state and the state in the news article? What other states or bodies of water border the state? What information can you learn about this state by reading the article? Is there anything unique

about the geography, history, or culture of this state that contributed to the events of the news story? Do you think this same story or event could have taken place in another state?

California rescuers free entangled whale	California
Boy scouts save leader from bear attack	New Jersey
Fossils of strange turtle found in Utah	Utah
Alaskan seabirds in trouble	Alaska
California condor returns to wild	California

- **Missing Words:** Select a number of articles. Remove one or two interesting words from each headline (see examples below). Display the incomplete headlines. Divide students into teams. Ask each team to come up with two possible completions for each headline: the most likely word and the funniest word. Give each team one of the articles to read together. Have each team stand and report on their assigned news article. Have the teams give a short summary of the article and then provide the correct missing word from the headline. Have the teams collect the responses from the other teams and give points for correct answers and their favorite funny answers.

    Archaeologists unearth centuries-old _____ in Bavaria

    The President hosts _____ festival at the White House

    Vermont college searches for missing _____

    SpaceX supply ship arrives at _____ with groceries

    Record for largest _____ set in Minnesota

    3 men see _____, free _____ buried in avalanche

Associated Press Articles Answer Key

Article Title	Q1	Q2	Q3	Q4
Grade 3				
How do you grow a 2,000-pound pumpkin? It's tricky	a	b	c	d
California rescuers free entangled whale	b	a	b	d
Boy Scouts save leader from bear attack	c	a, e	b, a, e, d, c	a
Trained elephants are helping control forest fires	d	c	b	a
Fossils of strange turtle found in Utah	b	b	b	c
Cliff-side full of fossils found in Utah	d	c	a, c	b
Alaskan seabirds in trouble	c	a	b	d
California condor returns to wild	d	d	a	a
More students learning computer science	a	b	a	d
London Zoo begins yearly animal count	c	c	a	d

Name: _____

How do you grow a 2,000-pound pumpkin? It's tricky

MICHELLE R. SMITH, The Associated Press
October 22, 2015
Lexile®: 620L, 167 words

COVENTRY, R.I. (AP) — Ron Wallace has a pumpkin patch in his backyard. And the pumpkins he grows are giant. He broke a world record in 2006. And in 2012, his prized pumpkin weighed 2,009 pounds.

Wallace has spent 27 years growing pumpkins. He conducts research and experiments with new ideas. He shares ideas with growers around the world.

Wallace believes that a good pumpkin comes from the best seeds. Top growers can trace their pumpkin seeds back many, many years.

Pumpkins can put on 45 pounds each day, mostly from water. The best pumpkins every year follow the weather. If the weather is just right, growers might see many huge pumpkins.

But these pumpkins won't end up in pumpkin pie. They're too big to be tasty.

Wallace took this season's biggest pumpkin to a weigh-off. It weighed a whopping 2,230 pounds. It was the second-biggest pumpkin ever grown.

Wallace wants to grow a 2,500-pound pumpkin next.

"I know my program is capable," he says. "We're gonna give it a shot."

How do you grow a 2,000-pound pumpkin? It's tricky

Comprehension Questions

1. **Choose the main idea of this article.**
   a. Ron Wallace breaks records with his giant pumpkins.
   b. Pumpkins grow very quickly.
   c. Large pumpkins do not make good pies.
   d. Ron Wallace helps people around the world grow pumpkins.

2. **Which statement from the article best supports the main idea?**
   a. He shares ideas with growers around the world.
   b. And in 2012, his prized pumpkin weighed 2,009 pounds.
   c. Pumpkins can put on 45 pounds each day, mostly from water.
   d. They're too big to be tasty.

3. **According to the article, what causes many huge pumpkins to grow?**
   a. a long season
   b. large seeds
   c. the right weather
   d. fresh soil

4. **Which detail from the article best supports the idea that Ron Wallace enjoys growing pumpkins?**
   a. His pumpkins are giant.
   b. He thinks he can grow a 2,500-pound pumpkin.
   c. He believes that good seeds produce good pumpkins.
   d. He has been growing pumpkins for 27 years.

Name: _____

California rescuers free entangled whale

GILLIAN FLACCUS, The Associated Press
November 1, 2015
Lexile®: 730L, 231 words

LONG BEACH, Calif. (AP) — Rescuers freed a humpback whale that was entangled in fishing line. The nylon rope stretched from its mouth to its tail.

The adult humpback was seen on Friday. It was about 45 miles south of Los Angeles.

The first rescue team cut about 100 feet of rope and buoys from the whale. But the whale became nervous and dove deep underwater. Rescuers couldn't reach it for the rest of the day.

The whale moved about 60 miles south. It was spotted again Saturday in San Diego.

The second rescue team was from a marine animal theme park. The team worked on helping the whale for three hours. They cut away more than 230 feet of rope.

A spokeswoman for the theme park said she hoped they gave the whale a second chance at life. She said a small amount of rope was left in the whale's mouth.

The first rescue team helped about 50 whales since January. A program specialist for the administration explained that warmer waters could be bringing the whales closer to shore. Here they get trapped in fishing gear.

The specialist said experts want to know how the whales are getting entangled.

Rescuers found information on the buoys. This information will help pinpoint where the whale became entangled.

Scientists are trying to think ahead. They are looking for ways to prevent whales from getting entangled in the future.

Imagine Learning®

Name: _____

California rescuers free entangled whale
Comprehension Questions

1. **Choose the main idea of this article.**
   a. Humpback whales can be found south of Los Angeles.
   b. Rescuers helped a humpback whale.
   c. Whales will eat things they should not eat.
   d. A whale can become nervous easily.

2. **Which detail from the article best supports the main idea?**
   a. Rescuers worked on the whale to remove rope.
   b. Some rope was left in the freed whale's mouth.
   c. The whale dove deep underwater when it became nervous.
   d. The adult humpback whale was seen about 45 miles south of Los Angeles.

3. **What caused the whale to get caught in the fishing line?**
   a. becoming nervous
   b. swimming close to shore
   c. moving 60 miles south
   d. diving deep underwater

4. **Which would be the best detail to add to this article?**
   a. the kinds of fish people catch off the California coast
   b. a list of whales that swim near the California coast
   c. a list of the types of rope used for fishing
   d. an idea that could keep whales from getting tangled in the future

Name: _____

Boy Scouts Save Leader From Bear Attack

The Associated Press
December 21, 2015
Lexile®: 670L, 217 words

ROCKAWAY TOWNSHIP, N.J. (AP) — A Boy Scout leader was pulled into a cave by a bear in New Jersey. He defended himself with a rock hammer while three Scouts called for help, authorities said.

Christopher Petronino and the Scouts were hiking at Split Rock Reservoir. Petronimo walked into a small opening in a cave, NJ.com reported. That's when the bear grabbed him by the foot. It yanked him inside and began biting his legs and shoulders.

Bob Considine is a spokesman for the state Department of Environmental Protection. He explained what happened next. Petronino defended himself with a rock hammer. He then pulled his sweatshirt over his head and curled into a ball. He yelled to the Scouts to get help.

The boys called 911. They were told to place food outside the cave to lure the bear away from Petronino. The plan worked.

"I want to commend those young Scouts," an official said. "They knew what to do."

Petronino said he'd visited the cave for decades and had never seen a bear.

State officials believe the bear was protecting its hibernation location. At first, they placed traps near the cave to capture the bear. Later they decided that the warmer weather was confusing the bears. Officials no longer believe the bear is a threat and won't try to capture it.

Name: _____

Boy Scouts save leader from bear attack
Comprehension Questions

1. **Choose the main idea of this article.**
   a. State officials set traps to capture the bear that attacked Christopher Petronino.
   b. Split Rock Reservoir is a dangerous place to go hiking.
   c. A Boy Scout leader was rescued from a bear by three Scouts.
   d. Calling 911 is a good plan if you find yourself in trouble.

2. **Which two details from the article best support the main idea?**
   a. Petronino yelled at the Scouts for help.
   b. Sometimes warm weather confuses bears.
   c. Petronino had been visiting the caves for many years and had never seen a bear.
   d. State officials believe the bear was protecting its hibernation location.
   e. The boys used food to get the bear out of its cave.

3. **Arrange the events from the article in the order in which they happened.**
   a. The bear dragged Petronino into the cave.
   b. The Scouts went hiking.
   c. The Scouts were commended for rescuing their leader.
   d. The bear left the cave to eat the food.
   e. The Scouts called 911.

4. **What evidence from the article explains why the bear is still free?**
   a. Officials no longer believe the bear is a threat.
   b. Petronino said he'd visited the cave for decades and had never seen a bear.
   c. State officials believe the bear was protecting its hibernation location.
   d. They were told to place food outside the cave to lure the bear away from Petronino.

Name: _____

Trained elephants are helping control forest fires

The Associated Press
November 11, 2015
Lexile®: 710L, 178 words

SIAK, Indonesia (AP) — Twenty-three trained elephants are being used in Indonesia to help control forest fires.

Riau province in East Sumatra has been covered in smoke for nearly three months. The smoke is from forest fires and land clearing. The province has many peat-rich areas. Peat burns very easily. It is very hard to control flames in these areas.

The trained elephants are being used as "forest watchdogs."

The elephants and their crews patrol burned areas in the forest. They carry water pumps and hoses. Their job is to make sure fires don't restart.

The elephants had earlier been trained in other ways. They helped find people that were on the land illegally. They also helped drive wild elephants out of human areas and back to their habitats.

Indonesia has had less rain than usual this year. People have also been burning the land. So Indonesia has been unable to put out the forest fires.

Much of the burned land has been turned into oil palm and pulp plantations. More than 25,000 acres of land have been burned in the province.

Imagine Learning·

Name: _____

Trained elephants are helping control forest fires

Comprehension Questions

1. **Choose the main idea of this article**
   a. East Sumatra is filled with smoke from fires.
   b. Elephants are easily trained.
   c. Indonesia needs more rain.
   d. Elephants are helping to control fires in Indonesia.

2. **Which detail from the article best supports the main idea?**
   a. One area has been covered in smoke for nearly three months.
   b. Indonesia didn't have as much rain this year as it needed.
   c. The elephants' job is to make sure fires don't start again.
   d. Many thousands of acres of land have been burned in the province.

3. **After reading the article, what can you infer about elephants?**
   a. They are afraid of fire.
   b. They are smart.
   c. They are slow-moving animals.
   d. They are not normally found in Indonesia.

4. **Which sentence correctly describes a problem and solution from the article?**
   a. Fires are stopped by trained elephants.
   b. Smoke is cleared with peat.
   c. Burned land is cleared by rain.
   d. Wild elephants are calmed by clearing the land.

Name: _____

Fossils of strange turtle found in Utah

The Associated Press
October 21, 2015
Lexile®: 780L, 233 words

SALT LAKE CITY (AP) — A strange pig-snouted turtle has been discovered in southern Utah.

The University of Utah announced the finding on Wednesday. A team from the Natural History Museum of Utah dug up the fossils. The turtle was discovered in the Grand Staircase-Escalante National Monument.

The strange-looking turtle was 2-feet long. It had a pig-like nose with two nostrils. Researchers say it is unlike any other turtle ever found.

The turtle lived about 76 million years ago during the Cretaceous Period. At this time, southern Utah had rivers and bayous. The climate was wet and hot. The turtle lived alongside Tyrannosaurs and duck-billed dinosaurs.

Joshua Lively is a student at the University of Texas. He studied the turtle's fossils for school. He called it one of the weirdest turtles that ever lived.

The findings were published in the Journal of Vertebrate Paleontology.

Name: _____

Fossils of strange turtle found in Utah
Comprehension Questions

1. **Choose the main idea of this article.**
   a. Many strange animals lived long ago.
   b. Unusual turtle fossils were found in Utah.
   c. Utah has changed over the years.
   d. Turtles are strange animals.

2. **Which detail from the article best supports the main idea?**
   a. The turtle that was found was 2-feet long.
   b. The pig-snouted turtle is unlike any other turtle ever found.
   c. Southern Utah had rivers and bayous 76 million years ago.
   d. The pig-snouted turtle lived at the same time as the other dinosaurs.

3. **Read this sentence from the article: "Joshua Lively is a student at the University of Texas."**
   What is the meaning of "university"?
   a. state
   b. school
   c. home
   d. center

4. **Joshua Lively called the turtle one of the weirdest turtles that ever lived because it**
   _____.
   a. was found in Utah
   b. lived in a wet and hot place
   c. had a pig-like nose with two nostrils
   d. lived at the same time as duck-billed dinosaurs

Name: _____

Cliff-side full of fossils found in Utah

BRADY McCOMBS ,The Associated Press
October 16, 2015
Lexile®: 640L, 245 words

SALT LAKE CITY (AP) — Paleontologists have discovered a cliff-side in Utah full of fossils. The fossils are from the Triassic Period. This is the beginning of the age of reptiles.

Among the discoveries is a new pterosaur. A pterosaur was a kind of dinosaur that could fly. It flew over a desert about 210 million years ago. It would have been the largest flying reptile of the time. Each side of its powerful lower jaw had two fangs and 28 ferocious teeth. It ate small crocodile-type creatures.

"If you saw one of these things coming at you with its jaws open, it would freak you out of your mind," said one paleontologist.

Most pterosaur fossils have been found crushed. But these fossils are in one piece.

Another paleontologist explained that it is rare to find small skeletons. It is unheard of to find them from the Triassic.

Eight animals have been identified at the site. They are most likely all new discoveries. One is a reptile with a head like a bird, arms like a mole, and a claw on its tail. Two are meat-eating dinosaurs. There are also small crocodile-like creatures with back armor.

The site is "in a time and a place that we really do not have a good record of," a different paleontologist said.

It was discovered by two paleontologists. They've found 11,500 bones so far. They are not nearly finished.

"This is the best stuff I'll ever see in my life," said one paleontologist.

Name: _____

Cliff-side full of fossils found in Utah
Comprehension Questions

1. **Choose the main idea of this article.**
   a. Flying dinosaurs lived during the Triassic Period.
   b. Paleontologists work to find the bones of unusual animals.
   c. The Triassic Period was the beginning of the age of reptiles.
   d. An exciting fossil site has been discovered in Utah.

2. **Which statement from the article best supports the main idea?**
   a. It would have been the largest flying reptile of the time.
   b. "If you saw one of these things coming at you with its jaws open, it would freak you out of your mind," said one paleontologist.
   c. "This is the best stuff I'll ever see in my life," said one paleontologist.
   d. It was discovered by two paleontologists.

3. **Which two details from the article best support the idea that the Utah discovery is an important one?**
   a. The pterosaur fossils are in one piece.
   b. The site was discovered by two paleontologists.
   c. The eight animals are most likely all new discoveries.
   d. The pterosaur ate small crocodile-type creatures.
   e. Paleontologists have discovered a cliff-side in Utah full of fossils.

4. **The pterosaur's strong jaws most likely helped it _____.**
   a. dig for food in the Utah desert
   b. bite through a crocodile creature's back armor
   c. live beyond the Triassic Period
   d. chew and grind the leaves of plants

Comprehension Questions: Cliff-side full of fossils found in Utah
Copyright © Imagine Learning, Inc.

Name: _____

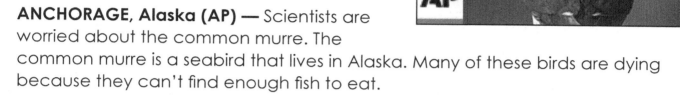

Alaskan seabirds in trouble

Dan Joling, The Associated Press
January 12, 2016
Lexile®: 780L, 220 words

ANCHORAGE, Alaska (AP) — Scientists are worried about the common murre. The common murre is a seabird that lives in Alaska. Many of these birds are dying because they can't find enough fish to eat.

Scientists suspect it has something to do with warming of the ocean on Alaska's coast. The fish that the common murres depend on for food live in a narrow band of cool water. As the water becomes warm, the fish leave to find cooler water. This leaves the birds without food.

Each spring, murres nest next to one another on cliffs and slopes. The females lay eggs in the shape of light bulbs. If the eggs roll, they roll in a circle instead of off the cliff.

Murres have short, powerful wings and are very good at swimming. They can dive deep in the water to hunt for fish.

These black and white birds look a bit like a penguin. This summer Alaskans reported seeing what looked like "skinny penguins" walking in roadways. Many of the females this year were too weak to lay their eggs.

Many starving murres ended up at the Bird Learning and Treatment Center. The center is located in Alaska's largest city, Anchorage.

The upcoming year doesn't look any better for the common murre. Scientists predict that the oceans worldwide will continue to be warm.

Alaskan seabirds in trouble
Comprehension Questions

1. **Choose the main idea of this article.**
   a. Many common murres went to the Bird Learning and Treatment Center for help.
   b. Scientists predict that oceans throughout the world will continue to be warm.
   c. The common murres are suffering because they don't have enough food.
   d. The fish eaten by the common murres leave the warm water to find cooler water.

2. **Which detail from the article best supports the main idea?**
   a. The fish the common murres eat are leaving the Alaska coast.
   b. Scientists are trying to figure out how to help the common murre.
   c. Murres are good at swimming because of their powerful wings.
   d. Many of the birds were too weak to lay their eggs.

3. **What statement from the text supports the claim that the murres will continue to be in trouble?**
   a. The center is located in Alaska's largest city, Anchorage.
   b. Scientists predict that the oceans worldwide will continue to be warm.
   c. This summer Alaskans reported seeing what looked like "skinny penguins" walking in roadways.
   d. The females lay eggs in the shape of light bulbs.

4. **What additional effect is likely to be caused by warming water?**
   a. The Bird Learning and Treatment Center will shut down.
   b. People in Alaska will see more penguins than usual.
   c. More common murre eggs will roll off of cliffs and into the water.
   d. The fish will also suffer because they will not be able to find cooler water.

Name: _____

California condor returns to wild

ELLEN KNICKMEYER, The Associated Press
January 1, 2016
Lexile®: 780L, 236 words

SAN FRANCISCO (AP) — After about 30 years in captivity, a male California condor flew back into the wild. The bird, named AC-4, was part of a captive program to help save the species. The program took place at the Bitter Creek National Wildlife Refuge in California.

AC-4 took a few minutes to get its bearings. Then biologist Joseph Brandt watched it fly out of its pen and glide over the canyon. It was the bird's first free flight since 1985. AC-4 had been one of just 23 condors left in the world in the 1980s.

"He kind of flew right past us. It was really incredible," Brandt said.

The California condor is North America's largest species of land bird. It has a wing span of over 9 feet.

So what drove the California condor toward extinction? Lead poisoning is believed to be one of the main factors. The birds eat pieces of lead bullets when they feed on animals shot by hunters.

California lawmakers voted to phase out lead bullets for hunting by 2019.

AC-4 is the father of the first chick born in the program. This gave the program hope they could save the species.

AC-4 is now the father of 30 condor chicks. The chicks have all been released into the wild.

Biologists recorded 19 wild condor nests in central and Southern California this year. That is more nests than at any point this century, Brandt said.

Name: _____

California condor returns to wild
Comprehension Questions

1. **Choose the main idea of this article.**
   a. In 1985 there were only 23 California condors left in all the world.
   b. The California condor is the largest bird in North America.
   c. One California condor has a wingspan of about 9 feet.
   d. A program to save the California condor is having success.

2. **Which detail from the article best supports the main idea?**
   a. AC-4 was kept at Bitter Creek National Wildlife Refuge in California.
   b. It was the bird's first free flight since 1985.
   c. The program was hopeful when the first chick was born.
   d. Biologists have found 19 more California condor nests this year.

3. **"AC-4 took a few minutes to get its bearings. Then biologist Joseph Brandt watched it fly out of its pen and glide over the canyon. It was the bird's first free flight since 1985."**
   What is another way of saying "to get its bearings"?
   a. To understand that it was free to fly wherever it wanted
   b. To remember how to glide through the air
   c. To see Joseph Brandt standing next to its pen
   d. To look for other condors in the California wildlife refuge

4. **What sentence correctly describes the problem and solution in the article?**
   a. California condors were in danger of disappearing from the earth until they were taken to the Bitter Creek National Wildlife Refuge for protection.
   b. Joseph Brant had never seen a California Condor fly until he watched AC-4 leave the Bitter Creek National Wildlife Refuge.
   c. Because of predators, California condors build their nests in caves high in the mountains or on the sides of cliffs.
   d. There are hundreds of wildlife refuges all over the country and about 45 million people visit them each year.

Name: _____

More students learning computer science

PHUONG LE, The Associated Press
December 2, 2015
Lexile®: 750L, 173 words

MARYSVILLE, Wash. (AP) — Six-year-old Lauren Meek drags and drops a block of code to build instructions. She clicks the "run" button and watches the characters move through a maze.

"Yes! This is so easy," says Meek. She is a kindergartener at Marshall Elementary.

Most elementary school students in her school district are getting weekly computer science lessons. This is part of a national effort to introduce more children to computer science.

Supporters say it's about learning how computers work. They say computer science teaches kids to think and be creative. It introduces them to the technology that will change their future.

More jobs need computer science, one researcher said. And computing is everywhere. That's why children need to understand it.

But a big problem is finding enough teachers who know how to teach computer science.

Computer science is not taught enough in schools today. However, colleges want to see students better prepared, said Terry Redican of The College Board.

One principal thinks of computer science as an opportunity. Learning computer science opens the door to jobs.

AP Articles: More students learning computer science
Copyright © Imagine Learning, Inc.

More students learning computer science
Comprehension Questions

1. **Choose the main idea of this article.**

    a. More students are learning computer science.

    b. Computing is everywhere.

    c. Principal Kelly Sheward likes computer science.

    d. Kindergarten students can play many games on a computer.

2. **Which statement from the article best supports the main idea?**

    a. Learning computer science opens the door to jobs.

    b. Six-year-old Lauren Meek drags and drops a block of code to build instructions.

    c. More jobs need computer science, one researcher said.

    d. But a big problem is finding enough teachers who know how to teach computer science.

3. **Read this sentence from the article: "Learning computer science opens the door to jobs." What does the phrase "opens the door to jobs" mean?**

    a. helps people get jobs

    b. teaches people about jobs

    c. creates more jobs for people

    d. brings jobs into people's homes

4. **Which statement from the article best supports the idea that even young children can be good at learning computer science?**

    a. And computing is everywhere.

    b. Learning computer science opens the door to jobs.

    c. One principal thinks of computer science as an opportunity.

    d. "Yes! This is so easy," said Meek.

Name: _____

London Zoo begins yearly animal count

The Associated Press
January 4, 2016
Lexile®: 760L, 132 words

London (AP) — London Zoo began its yearly census Monday. Animals walked, swam, crawled or flew to be counted.

Zookeepers used cameras, calculators and clipboards to count the critters. They plan to record every mammal, bird, fish, invertebrate, reptile and amphibian in the zoo. The census will take one week to finish.

The zoo is home to 17,500 animals of more than 750 species. The animals include large silverback gorillas down to tiny leaf-cutter ants. New this year are a baby Western lowland gorilla and African hunting dog pups.

Ants and other tiny creatures are counted in colonies. All others are counted one by one.

The census is required by all British zoos. The data is used for zoo management. It is also used for special programs. Some of these programs help protect endangered animals.

Name: _____

London Zoo begins yearly animal count
Comprehension Questions

1. **Choose the main idea of this article.**
   a. London Zoo has 750 species of animals.
   b. Animal census data is used for special programs and animal protection.
   c. All the animals at London Zoo are counted during one week each year.
   d. Zookeepers used cameras during the census.

2. **Which detail from the article best supports the main idea?**
   a. There are several new animals living at the zoo this year.
   b. The information they collect is used for zoo management.
   c. Zookeepers plan to record every animal in the zoo.
   d. Endangered animals are protected by special programs.

3. **Read this sentence from the article: "London Zoo began its yearly census Monday." What is the meaning of "census"?**
   a. counting and collecting information about a group
   b. bringing all the zoo animals for a checkup at the vet
   c. looking at data to decide which new animals to get
   d. creating a special program for endangered animals

4. **After reading the article, why is the census important?**
   a. Zookeepers should finish the census in less than one week.
   b. The census is required by all British zoos and is done every year.
   c. Zoo management learns about new baby animals after the census.
   d. Census information is used for zoo management and to protect animals.

 Imagine Learning

Notes

Comprehension Strategies Guide

Resource Overview

Comprehension Strategies texts and printouts help students learn strategies such as comparing and contrasting information, identifying the main idea and supporting details, and charting story structure. Along with the story texts, blank Graphic Organizers for each comprehension strategy are provided to support students by helping them to visualize connections and relationships between facts, information, and terms. Completed model Graphic Organizers accompany each text printout.

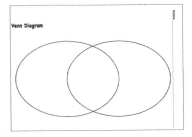

The **Main Idea Graphic Organizer** can be used to identify the main or central idea of an informational text as well as the details that support the main idea.

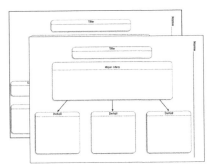

The **Story Map Graphic Organizer** can be used to help students identify the characters, setting, problems, and solution/resolution of a story. One version includes only the problem; another version also includes the plot.

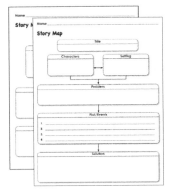

The **Compare/Contrast Graphic Organizer** can be used to help students to classify, identify characteristics, and show how two ideas, stories, or texts are alike and different.

Online Resource Overview

Project Imagine Learning's online instructional comprehension strategies activities to teach or review the concepts of story map, main idea, and compare/contrast prior to practicing with the printouts.

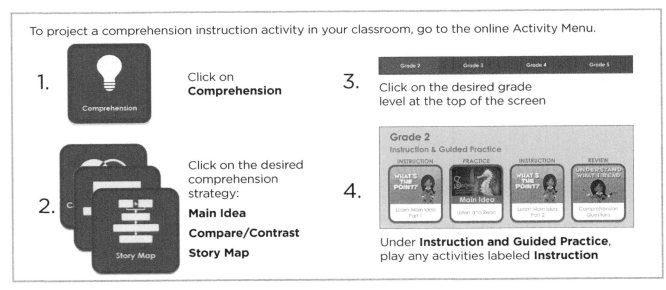

To project a comprehension instruction activity in your classroom, go to the online Activity Menu.

1. Click on **Comprehension**

2. Click on the desired comprehension strategy:

   Main Idea

   Compare/Contrast

   Story Map

3. Click on the desired grade level at the top of the screen

4. Under **Instruction and Guided Practice**, play any activities labeled **Instruction**

Imagine Learning

How to Use This Resource in the Classroom

- **Pre-read:** Use graphic organizers to preview ideas, relationships, or sequences and prepare students for important concepts they will encounter in the text.

- **Prewrite:** Have students use a graphic organizer to brainstorm and map plots, sequences, or relationships between a main idea and its details. This will help students narrow down and organize their ideas before beginning the writing process.

- Have students complete the Graphic Organizer. Depending on group size, consider the following processes:

  - **Whole class:** Distribute the text printout and Graphic Organizer. Project the graphic organizer. Review each term or element as needed. Ask the students to listen for these elements as you read the text together out loud. Have students raise their hand as they identify information that can go in the Graphic Organizer. Have students fill out their individual printouts as you model it. When finished reading, review the graphic organizer. Discuss the text and fill in any additional information.

  - **Small Groups:** Display and review the selected graphic organizer. Tell students the name and main idea of the text, or preview the plot of the story. Brainstorm with students to predict details they think might go in the completed Graphic Organizer. Divide students into small groups of three to five students and assign reader and writer roles to the members of the group. Give the text printout to the readers and the Graphic Organizer to the writers. Have the readers take turns reading a paragraph or section at a time aloud to the group. Have students discuss each section as they read. Ask the writers to record details from the discussion on the Graphic Organizer. Once students have finished, have groups report to the class the results of their discussion. Point out and discuss commonalities or distinct differences among group results.

  - **Guided Pairs:** Project or display the Graphic Organizer. Review elements and details as needed. Pair students with a partner. Give each pair a text printout and Graphic Organizer. Have the students read just the first section of text aloud with their partner. Have students work together to apply the comprehension strategy. Review answers and model filling out the Graphic Organizer. Then have the students read the remaining sections of the text, completing their Graphic Organizer as they read. When they are finished reading, have partners discuss the text and make corrections or add details to the graphic organizer. Lead a group discussion to review answers and compare results. Display or project the completed model Graphic Organizer as needed during the discussion.

  - **Independent Pairs:** Pair students with a partner. Give each pair a text printout and the corresponding Graphic Organizer. Have students take turns reading the text aloud with their partner, pausing to fill out the Graphic Organizer as they read. When they finish reading, have partners discuss the text and add any necessary details to the Graphic Organizer. Have students use the completed model Graphic Organizer to check their comprehension.

  - **Individual:** As necessary, review elements and details of the comprehension strategy. Provide student with a text printout and the corresponding Graphic Organizer. Ask students to first review the Graphic Organizer printout and be prepared to look for these elements as they read the text on their own. Have students fill in the details as they read. Have students use the completed model Graphic Organizer to check their comprehension when they have finished reading the story. Extend learning by having them present and explain their Graphic Organizer to a partner or by having volunteers explain each section of the Graphic Organizer to the class.

- **Summarize:** After reading, have students use graphic organizers to summarize information such as cause and effect factors or main ideas and supporting details. The visual nature of the graphic organizer will help students follow processes, make inferences, and draw conclusions.

Classroom Activities

Name _____

Story Map

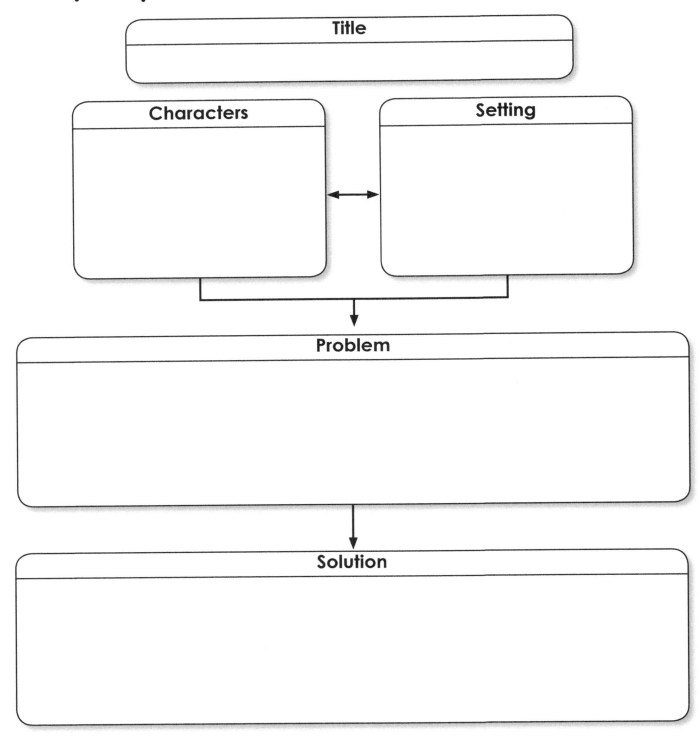

Title

Characters

Setting

Problem

Solution

Story Map Printout 1
Copyright © Imagine Learning, Inc.

Name_____

Story Map

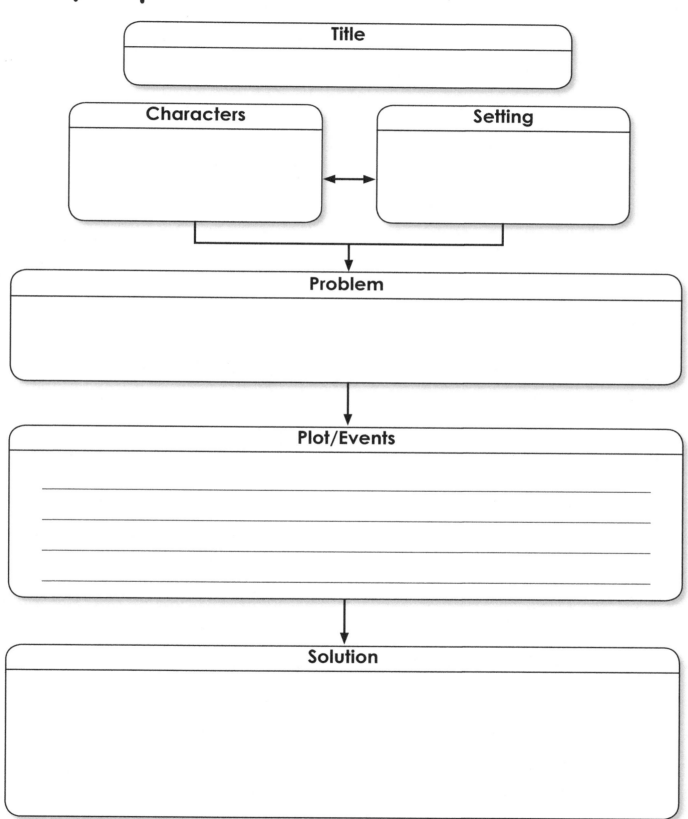

Title

Characters	Setting

↔

Problem

Plot/Events

Solution

Name _____

Title

Main Idea

Detail

Detail

Detail

Main Idea Printout 1
Copyright © Imagine Learning, Inc.

Name_____

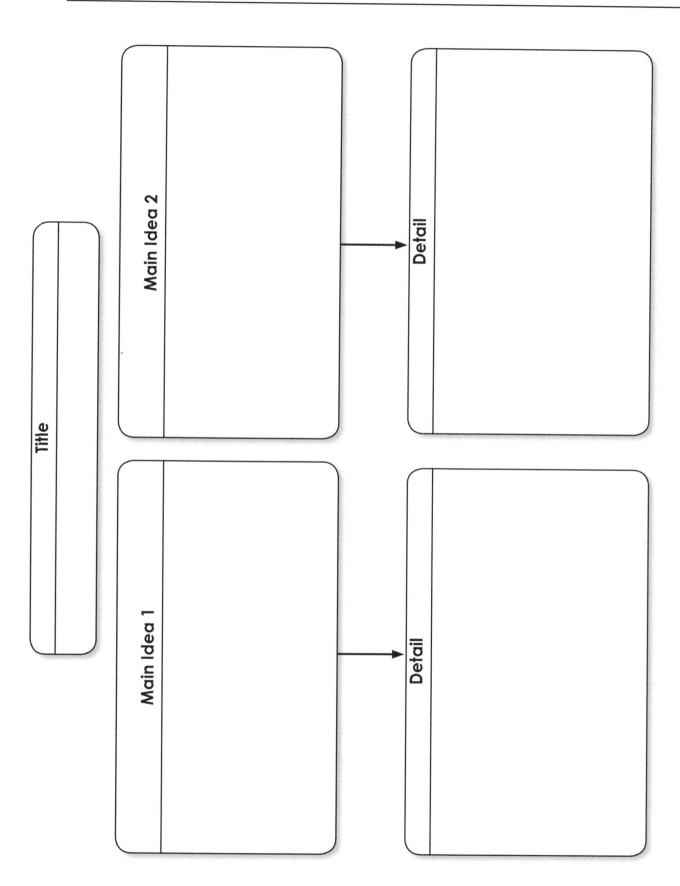

Title

Main Idea 2

Main Idea 1

Detail

Detail

Name _____

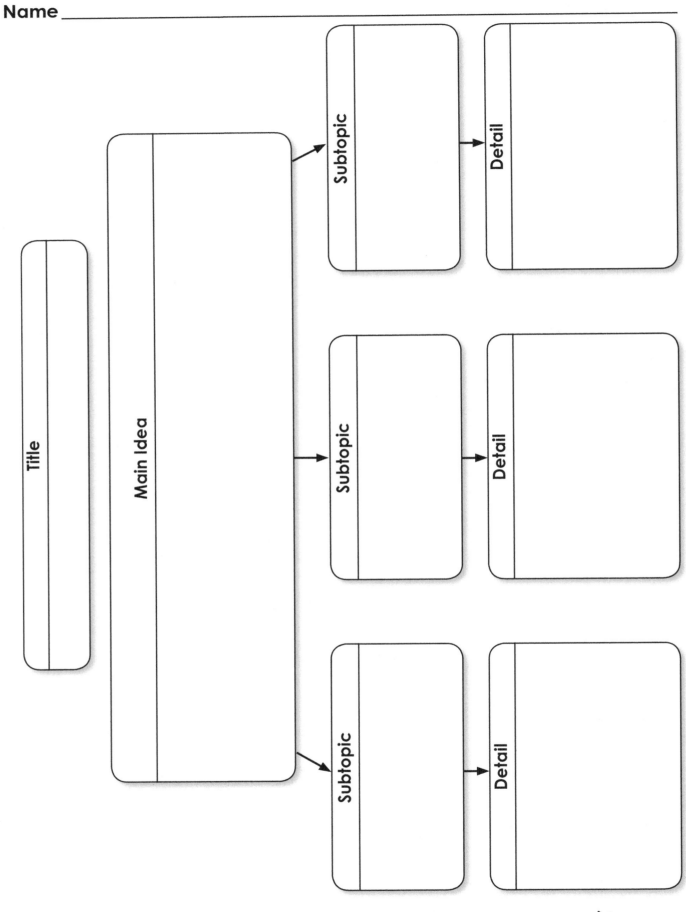

Title

Main Idea

Subtopic → Detail

Subtopic → Detail

Subtopic → Detail

Main Idea Printout 3
Copyright © Imagine Learning, Inc.

Name: _____

Title

Main Idea 2

Subtopic

Subtopic

Detail

Detail

Main Idea 1

Subtopic

Subtopic

Detail

Detail

 Imagine Learning®

Main Idea Printout 4
Copyright © Imagine Learning, Inc.

Name _____

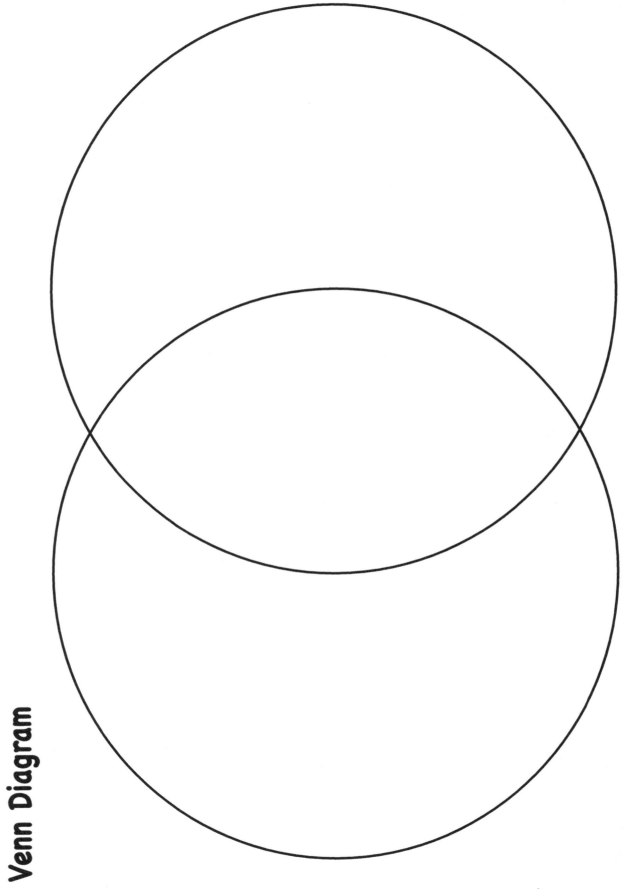

Venn Diagram

Venn Diagram Printout
Copyright © Imagine Learning, Inc.

Name: _____

The Boy Who Cried Wolf

Compare and Contrast (Literature)
Grade 2, Story 1

Lexile®: 470L, 338 words

Once upon a time, there was a boy who had a very important job. Every day, he had to sit on a hill and watch the town's sheep to make sure they were safe. There was only one problem. He thought watching sheep was the most boring job ever.

The boy was so bored that he had to do something to make things more exciting. What would be exciting? The boy had an idea, and he ran to town as fast as he could. He yelled, "Wolf! Hey, there's a wolf up there!"

People came out into the street. "What? A wolf!" They ran out of town and up the hill, but there was no wolf. The people were angry with the boy. They told him to only cry "wolf!" if the sheep were in real danger.

But the next day was so boring that the boy ran to town again. "Wolf!" he yelled.

"This better not be a trick," the people told him. They ran all the way up the hill to see. There were the sheep, but there was no wolf. The angry people again told the boy that what he did was wrong, but, as soon as they were gone, he laughed and laughed.

On the third day, the boy started looking for something to do when he saw a big, black shape coming toward him. It was a wolf!

The boy ran into town. "Wolf," he gasped. "There's a wolf!" The people did not believe him.

The people did not follow him.

Then one old man spoke, "I think this boy has learned his lesson. Let's give him one more chance. I don't want a wolf to take our sheep."

Finally, the people followed the boy. The wolf had almost reached the herd. The people ran to the sheep just in time to scare the wolf away.

That night, the boy told all the townspeople he was sorry. "I think," he said, "that watching sheep is not boring after all."

Imagine Learning®

Name: _____

The Wolf Who Cried Boy

Compare and Contrast (Literature)
Grade 2, Story 2

Lexile®: 450L, 337 words

Once upon a time, there was a young wolf who spent his days in the forest under the trees. His job was to watch for boys. The wolf pack was afraid of boys because some boys hunted wolves. So the young wolf watched and waited in the forest, but no boys came. There was nothing to do. He was bored.

Bored, bored, bored. He tried to think of something to make life more exciting, and then he had an idea.

"Boy!" he yelled. "There's a boy in the forest. Run for your lives!"

All the wolves were afraid and ran away. The young wolf laughed and laughed at how silly they looked.

The wolves were angry. They told the young wolf to never cry "boy!" unless a real boy had come. The young wolf didn't listen.

The next day, he was bored again. "Help! I saw a boy, and he almost got me!" he yelled.

The wolf pack thought it must be true, so they ran off again.

When they found out the truth, the wolf pack was very angry. They said, "Never lie again."

"The young wolf walked around the forest the next day, still laughing at how he had tricked the pack. Suddenly, he smelled something . . . and then he heard something . . . and finally he saw something. It was a boy!

The young wolf raced home. "A boy!" he cried. "It's really a boy this time!"

Name: _____

No one believed him.

The young wolf didn't know what to do. He ran away, but he ran the wrong way—right into the boy!

"What are you doing?" the boy asked as he rubbed his head.

"I was running away," the young wolf said. "Aren't you here to shoot wolves?"

"Yes," the boy told him, "I want to shoot as many as I can." He reached behind his back.

"Help!" screamed the wolf, so scared that he couldn't even move.

"Now just hold still," said the boy as he brought out his camera. "I want to shoot your photo."

Click.

Name_____

Venn Diagram

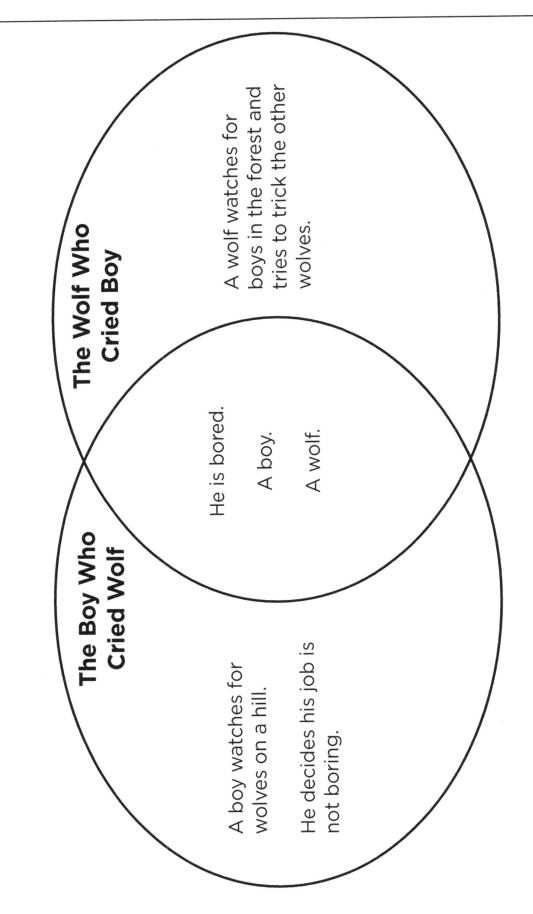

The Wolf Who Cried Boy

A wolf watches for boys in the forest and tries to trick the other wolves.

He is bored.

A boy.

A wolf.

The Boy Who Cried Wolf

A boy watches for wolves on a hill.

He decides his job is not boring.

Venn Diagram: The Boy Who Cried Wolf and The Wolf Who Cried Boy
Copyright © Imagine Learning, Inc.

✗ Imagine Learning®

Name: _____

The Fossil Hunter

Compare and Contrast (Literature)
Grade 3, Story 1

Lexile®: 700L, 486 words

I can't believe that I have to stay with Aunt Megan. She's really nice, but she always wants me to go to work with her. She's a ranger at a big state park called Fossil Butte. She spends all day hiking up and down trails and showing people around. My idea of a good time is to stay inside and play video games.

Aunt Megan thinks it will be good for me to spend the whole day outside enjoying the fresh air. What do I think? I think that walking for miles and miles will be very boring.

She wants me to find a fossil. How do you find a fossil? Aunt Megan says I need to investigate rocks very carefully. Looking at rocks is not fun.

But the sooner I find a fossil, the sooner I can get back to my video games. I keep my eyes open, but all I see is regular old rocks.

We're pretty high up the mountain now, heading into the trees. Aunt Megan shows me jagged lines scratched into the trees where mountain lions have sharpened their claws. I have to admit, it would be cool to see a mountain lion. I look around. Aunt Megan is gone.

"Come on up here!"

I breathe a big sigh of relief. Aunt Megan is not a mountain lion's dinner. I scramble up toward the top of the mountain and toward Aunt Megan.

Since a lot of paleontologists have already been here searching for fossils, I doubt that I will ever find one. I look down. I can't believe that this was once a huge lake full of fish and tropical plants and even alligators.

I'm trying to imagine an alligator climbing this mountain. Then I see something through the trees that looks like rock on the ground with faint

marks on it. As I get closer, I can hardly believe what I see. A fish fossil! That little fish was hiding there in the rock for maybe a million years until I found it.

"Have you discovered anything yet?" Aunt Megan calls. "If we don't hurry, you'll miss your favorite TV show."

"Who cares about TV? You won't believe what I just found."

The Fossil Hunter (Grade 3)
Copyright © Imagine Learning, Inc.

Name: _____

City Search

Compare and Contrast (Literature)
Grade 3, Story 2

Lexile®: 680L, 533 words

"What do you think?" Dad asked as he looked over Jade's shoulder.

Jade looked at the schedule one more time to make sure. "I think that we should take the 8:55 train. Then we can get off at 83rd Street."

Dad nodded. "Good job reading the schedule; we'll get there in no time with you in charge. Have you decided what to get for your brother once we're there?"

Jade shook his head, and his shoulders slumped a little.

"Cheer up—we'll find something that's just right for him." Dad walked with Jade to the right train. While they waited to get on, they chatted about what they might find for Martin's birthday.

Once on the train, the world zoomed by just like the birthday ideas zoomed through Jade's head.

At the station on 83rd, they got out and walked toward the sports shop. "Maybe we should get Martin a baseball hat or a sweatshirt," Dad said. "He would love some kind of baseball gift."

"Maybe," Jade said, but he was thinking that he needed something better than a sweatshirt. Dozens of sweatshirts hung on the rack, and they all looked the same. Jade wanted to get Martin something special.

When they left the sports store, Jade noticed a bus stop across the street. He pulled out their bus schedule.

"Look, Dad. We could catch the 9:45 bus to Charleston Street." There were plenty of stores on Charleston Street, but Jade was thinking of one store in particular.

They boarded the bus, rode for a few blocks, and then got off at their stop. Jade began walking toward a pet shop when his dad gently stopped him.

"I'm sorry, Jade, but Martin can't have a pet. Pets aren't allowed in his apartment building."

"Not even a fish?"

Dad shook his head and then said, "We can get on the trolley and go to a bookstore. Martin needs a break sometimes at college, and he might like a fun book." Jade shrugged, checked the schedule, and found a trolley that would be going past soon.

When they got to the store, Jade held his breath. What if they ran out of time before finding something for Martin's birthday?

He looked through the mysteries, adventure stories, and graphic novels, but he couldn't find anything that was just right. He needed something Martin was interested in. Something he would enjoy. But also something different and one-of-a-kind.

Out of the corner of his eye, Jade noticed a group of people. They looked excited, and he wondered what could be so interesting at a bookstore.

A lady who worked there was telling customers about a new book that they could have signed by the author. "In fact," she told them, "this specific book is about baseball, so both the author and a major league baseball player are here to sign copies of it."

Jade walked forward as if a magnet were pulling him. There sat a real author and a real baseball player together at the same table.

Jade grabbed his dad's arm. "Dad, we have to get it for Martin."

Dad smiled and said, "Let's get in line. I have a feeling that you found the perfect gift."

Venn Diagram

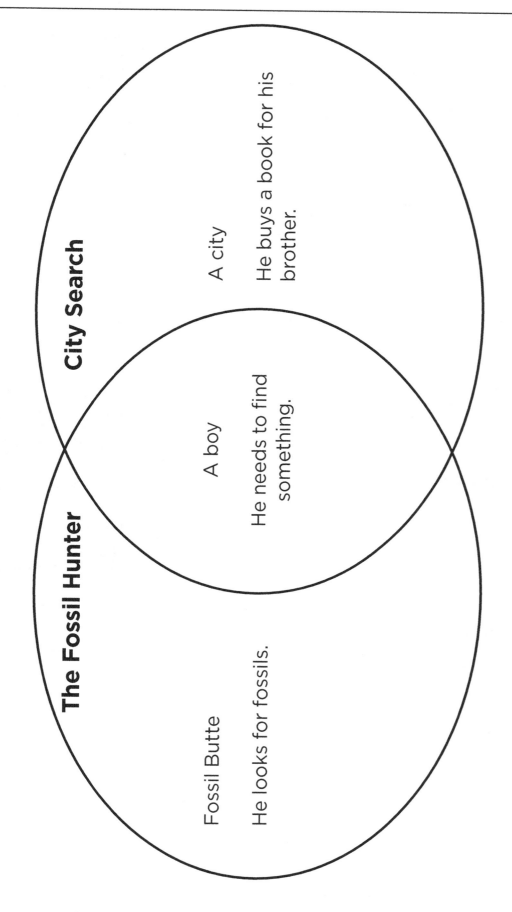

City Search

A city

He buys a book for his brother.

The Fossil Hunter

Fossil Butte

He looks for fossils.

A boy

He needs to find something.

Venn Diagram: The Fossil Hunter and City Search

Name: _____

My Painting

Compare and Contrast (Informational Text)

Grade 2, Article 1

Lexile®: 570L, 69 words

I love to paint. When I paint, I use my hands to hold the brush. I mix the paint to create my own colors. Then I dip the brush in my bright colors and swirl it onto the canvas. I create an animal from my imagination. I add details so that my animal is interesting to look at. I hang my painting on the wall when I am finished.

My Sculpture

Compare and Contrast (Informational Text)

Grade 2, Article 2

Lexile®: 590L, 59 words

I love to make sculptures. I use my hands to shape the clay. I squish and fold it to make different things. I use black and white clay to make an animal from real life. I carve details with my sculpting tool to give my animal a face. I put my sculpture on the table when I am finished.

Name_____

Venn Diagram

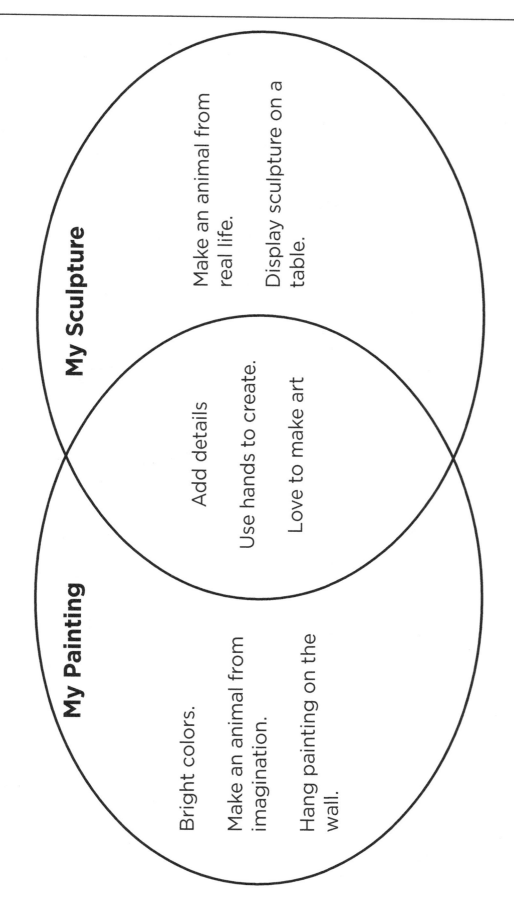

My Sculpture

Make an animal from real life.

Display sculpture on a table.

Add details

Use hands to create.

Love to make art

My Painting

Bright colors.

Make an animal from imagination.

Hang painting on the wall.

Name: _____

Reduce. Reuse. Recycle.

Compare and Contrast (Informational Text)
Grade 3, Article 1

Lexile®: 590L, 59 words

No one likes to see garbage on the ground. No one likes to see garbage filling up oceans and landfills, either. There's a lot you can do to help keep the earth clean.

Reduce

The best way to keep garbage from piling up is to limit how much you make. Think about how often you throw a box or wrapper away. Buy snacks that come in bulk instead of little snack bags. Help plant a garden so your family can eat fresh, unpackaged foods. When you use less packaging, you reduce the garbage you create.

Reuse

Need to buy something new? Try reusing what you have instead. Learn to sew and turn your old clothes into bags or toys. Save your plastic food containers for storing leftovers. Or decorate them. Then you can use them for holding toys or pens and pencils. Anything you do to keep your stuff out of the garbage will help the earth.

Recycle

Paper, plastic bags, bottles, and other items can be made into new stuff. Save your recyclables, and turn them in to your city's recycling center. You can even earn money by recycling soda cans and plastic bottles.

You can make a big difference by practicing the three Rs regularly!

Name: _____

Make Your Own Recycled Paper

Compare and Contrast (Informational Text)
Grade 3, Article 2

Lexile®: 700L, 190 words

Did you know that you can make your own recycled paper at home? Here's what you will need:

- newspaper, paper towels, or construction paper
- a dishpan
- a blender
- an 8 x 10 inch piece of small-holed screen
- a towel
- a smooth board
- a cotton cloth

Step 1:

Tear the paper into small pieces. Then fill a dishpan with warm water and soak the pieces in it all night.

Step 2:

The next day, add more warm water to the dishpan and break the mixture apart.

Step 3:

Place the mixture in your blender and add enough water to fill it halfway. Blend the mixture in short bursts until it looks like mushy soup. You've created pulp.

Step 4:

Cover the screen evenly with your pulp. Then lay a towel out and place the screen on top. Press the board firmly onto the pulp, squeezing out the water. Set the board aside when done.

Step 5:

Place the cotton cloth on a flat surface. Turn the screen over onto the cloth and carefully remove it, leaving the paper on the cloth. You may need to use a spatula to separate the paper from the screen.

Step 6:

Lay your paper out to dry. You can experiment by adding dried flowers, glitter, or other add-ins when creating your pulp. Just think of all the different kinds of paper you can make!

Name_____

Venn Diagram

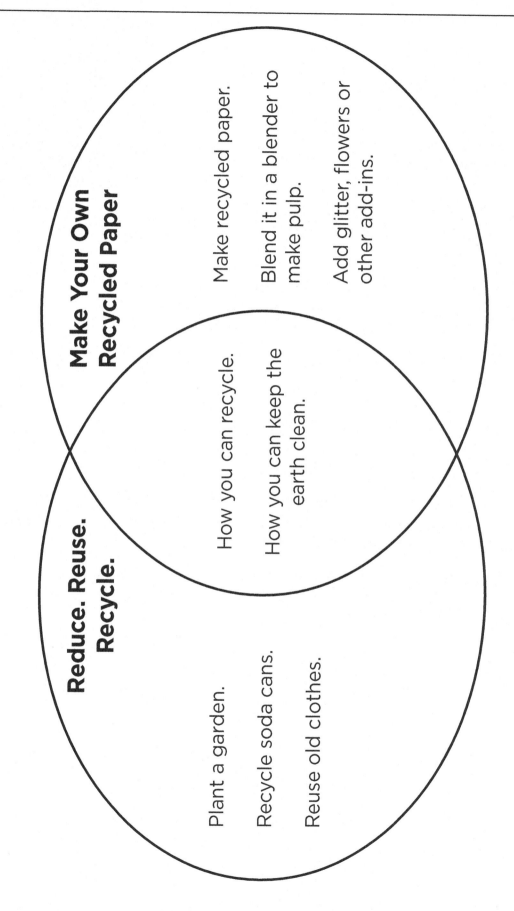

Make Your Own Recycled Paper

Make recycled paper.

Blend it in a blender to make pulp.

Add glitter, flowers or other add-ins.

Reduce. Reuse. Recycle.

How you can recycle.

How you can keep the earth clean.

Plant a garden.

Recycle soda cans.

Reuse old clothes.

✖ Imagine Learning®

Venn Diagram: Reduce. Reuse. Recycle. and Make Your Own Recycled Paper

Name: _____

Classroom Activities

Seahorses

Main Idea

Grade 2, Article 1

Written by Clydie Wakefield

Illustrated by Maryn Roos

Lexile®: 580L, 203 words

Have you ever seen a seahorse? If so, you have probably been amazed. A seahorse is a really cool fish. It has a head like a horse, a fin like a fish, and a tail like a monkey.

Sadly, seahorses are beginning to disappear. Millions are caught and used to make medicine. They are also sold as pets or souvenirs. And they are dying because their homes are disappearing.

Over 24 million seahorses are caught each year in order to make a Chinese medicine. This medicine is very popular. People believe it can cure a number of health problems.

Another several million are sold for home aquariums. It is difficult to keep these seahorses alive in a tank. Most of them die within a year. Seahorses are also popular as souvenirs. People buy dried seahorses as decorations.

Seahorses are also dying because their homes are disappearing. They live in seagrass beds in shallow waters. Many of these waters have become polluted. This pollution kills the seagrass beds.

Seahorses are disappearing every day. It isn't easy to find a live one. If you are lucky enough to see one, take a long look. You might not have many chances to see this amazing fish.

Name_____

Title

Seahorses

Main Idea

Seahorses are becoming extinct.

Detail

Seahorses are used as pets and decorations.

Detail

Seahorses are losing their homes because of pollution.

Detail

Seahorses are used for medicine.

 ImagineLearning®

Main Idea: Seahorses

Name: _____

How Do Seeds Get Around?

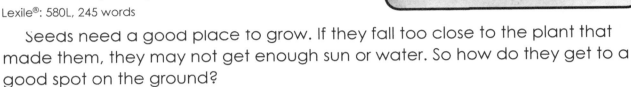

Main Idea

Grade 2, Article 2

Written by Clydie Wakefield
Illustrated by Maryn Roos

Lexile®: 580L, 245 words

Seeds need a good place to grow. If they fall too close to the plant that made them, they may not get enough sun or water. So how do they get to a good spot on the ground?

Some seeds travel a long way from where they start. In fact, some move miles away. How do they do it? They fly, float, or hitchhike.

Flying Seeds

Some seeds have wings like an airplane's. They glide through the air. The seed of an Asian climbing gourd has long wings. It glides in large, wide circles. Other seeds fly like a helicopter or drift like a parachute.

Floating Seeds

Some seeds float on water. A coconut palm tree may drop its seed into the ocean. The ocean current can carry it a long way. Sometimes the seed will travel 1,000 miles before it reaches dry land.

Hitchhiking Seeds

Some seeds travel by animal. Cocklebur plants make seeds covered with little hooks. These hooks grab onto the fur of passing animals. The seeds stay on an animal until they are scratched or pulled off. They might land far away from where they started.

Seeds can also travel *inside* animals. Seeds that animals eat end up in animal droppings. The seeds grow wherever the droppings land.

Plants create seeds that grow into new plants. But seeds need a good place to grow. They can fly, float, or hitchhike to get there. It's amazing how seeds can really get around!

Name _____

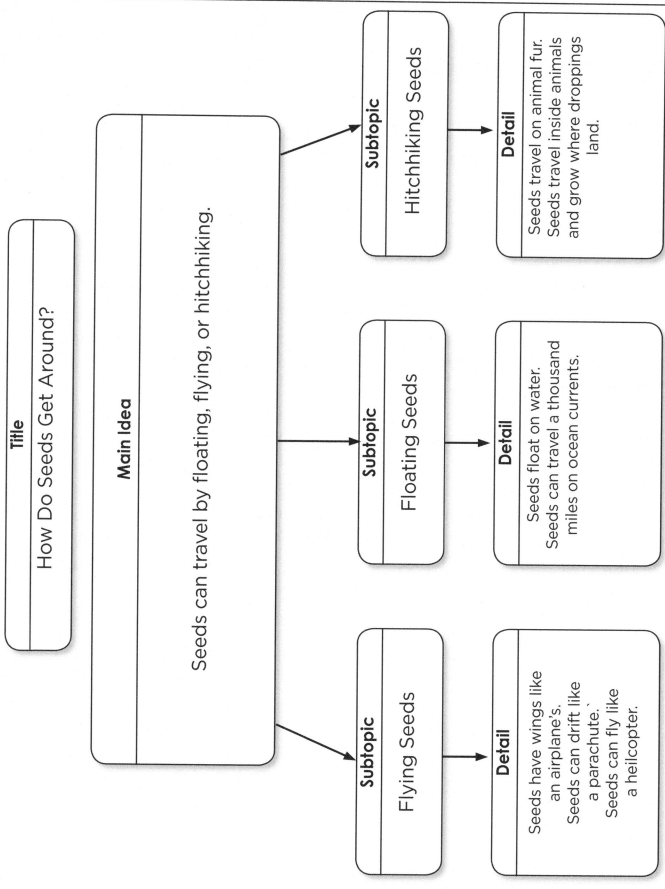

Title

How Do Seeds Get Around?

Main Idea

Seeds can travel by floating, flying, or hitchhiking.

Subtopic

Hitchhiking Seeds

Detail

Seeds travel on animal fur.
Seeds travel inside animals and grow where droppings land.

Subtopic

Floating Seeds

Detail

Seeds float on water.
Seeds can travel a thousand miles on ocean currents.

Subtopic

Flying Seeds

Detail

Seeds have wings like an airplane's.
Seeds can drift like a parachute.
Seeds can fly like a helicopter.

Main Idea: How Do Seeds Get Around?

Name: _____

Animal Hibernation

Main Idea
Grade 3, Article 1
Written by Michael Gravelle
Illustrated by Aaron Houston
Lexile®: 720L, 174 words

Animals need food so that they can have energy. They use that energy to move and stay warm.

But sometimes food can be hard to find, especially in winter. So some animals, like groundhogs and squirrels, have found a way to live through the cold winter by saving up their energy. It's called hibernation.

Before animals hibernate, they eat as much as they can. Their bodies turn the food into a layer of fat. The fat gives the animals all the energy they need while they're hibernating.

Since it takes a lot of energy to move, animals hold very still while they hibernate. In fact, hibernation looks a lot like sleeping. They're not sleeping, though. They're very carefully saving energy.

Remember how it also takes energy for mammals to stay warm? Well, when most animals hibernate, their body temperatures get very low. Some animals cool off so much that they're almost the same temperature as snow!

When the cold weather ends, the animals warm up and start moving and looking for food again.

Name_____

Title

Animal Hibernation

Main Idea

Animals hibernate to save energy during winter.

Detail

Before hibernating, animals eat a lot.

Detail

Animals lower their body temperatures when hiberanating.

Detail

Hibernating animals do not move very much.

Main Idea: Animal Hibernation

Name: _____

Gabriela Mistral

Main Idea

Grade 3, Article 2

Written by Naomi Pope

Illustrated by Tiffany LaGrange

Lexile®: 720L, 187 words

In 1889, Gabriela Mistral was born in a small village in Chile. During her life, Gabriela became one of Chile's most famous people. She was known for her talent, hard work, and desire to help people.

Gabriela was a very talented poet. Her first poems were published when she was only fifteen years old! Later, she became the first Latin American to win the biggest writing award in the world, the Nobel Prize for Literature.

But Gabriela wasn't just a great poet. When she was twelve, she started studying on her own to become a teacher. It was hard work, but it paid off!

Soon she was teaching children all over Chile. She even became a principal at the best school in the country.

Gabriela had many ideas that she wanted to share with the world. She spent a lot of her life visiting teachers and writers in other countries. She traveled to places like France, Puerto Rico, Brazil, and the United States.

Even though Gabriela Mistral traveled all over the world, the people of Chile never forgot her. They are still proud of her great accomplishments.

Name_____

Title

Gabriela Mistral

Main Idea

Gabriela Mistral is one of Chile's most famous people.

Subtopic

Teacher

Detail

Taught children all over Chile. Became a principal at the best school in the country.

Subtopic

Shared ideas with the world

Detail

Visited teachers and writers in other countries. Traveled to France Puerto Rico, Brazil, and the U.S.

Subtopic

Talented poet

Detail

Poems published at 15 years old. First Latin American to win the Nobel Prize for Literature.

Main Idea: Gabriela Mistral

Name: _____

Operation Hummingbird Rescue!

Story Map
Grade 2, Article 1
Written by Clydie Wakefield
Illustrated by Jim Madsen
Lexile®: 470L, 294 words

Maya looked up when she heard a loud thud against the window. *What was that?* she wondered. She walked over to take a closer look. A hummingbird was lying on the window ledge. Was it dead?

She called to her grandpa, "Abuelito, a hummingbird just crashed into our window!" Abuelito got up quickly and followed Maya outside.

"Is it going to be okay?" Maya asked. Abuelito studied the bird. Its eyes were open, but it didn't move.

"Don't touch it," he whispered. He slowly moved his hands toward the bird. It still didn't move.

"That's not good. I thought it would fly away," Abuelito said.

"Its wings don't look hurt," Maya said.

"You're right," Abuelito said. "Hmm...Let's see if it will drink something. Quick, go get the hummingbird feeder." Maya ran to get the feeder then rushed back to Abuelito.

Abuelito gently lifted the bird. He held it up to the feeder and slowly slid its beak in and out of the feeder port. "Look, Maya, I think it's drinking."

"How can you tell?" she asked.

"See how its throat is moving up and down? And watch the tip of its beak. Can you see it sticking its little tongue in and out?" Abuelito whispered.

"Does that mean it is going to be okay?" Maya asked.

Name: _____

"Let's see. Put on these gloves and hold out your hand," Abuelito said. When Maya held out her hand, Abuelito set the bird gently in the middle of it. The bird was there for just a second and then it was gone, whirring softly away. Abuelito and Maya looked at each other.

"You saved him, Abuelito!" Maya said.

Abuelito let out a long sigh and gave Maya a hug.

"We were just very lucky...and so was your hummingbird!"

Story Map

Title
Operation Rescue Hummingbird

Characters	Setting
Maya Abeulito A hummingbird	Maya's house

Problem
The hummingbird crashes into window.

Solution
Abuelito helps Maya feed the hummingbird and it flies away.

Story Map: Operation Hummingbird Rescue
Copyright © Imagine Learning, Inc.

Name: _____

Missing Homework

Story Map
Grade 2, Article 2

Written by Stacy Courtright
Illustrated by Maryn Roos
Lexile®: 510L, 317 words

Rosa finished her poster for her English project. She had glued a bunch of things on it. She thought it looked very cool. She titled it "My Favorite Things." Rosa put her poster on the kitchen table. She reached down to give her dog, Max, a pat on the head. Then she went to bed.

When Max saw the poster, he began running around in circles. He could not believe what was glued to it. It was Mr. Fuzzy, his favorite toy. Max jumped on the table. He bit into Mr. Fuzzy. Then he dragged the poster out the doggy door.

Rosa walked into the kitchen the next morning to check on her poster. It was missing! Panicked, she yelled, "Mom, I can't find my favorite things poster!"

"Where did you leave it?" Mom asked.

"On the kitchen table," Rosa said.

"What does it look like?" Mom asked.

"It has some of my favorite things glued to it," Rosa said.

"You glued your favorite things?" Mom cried.

"Well, I couldn't glue Max, so I glued his old toy, Mr. Fuzzy. I also included a daisy and pictures of you, Dad, and Joel," Rosa said.

Outside, Max chewed happily on Mr. Fuzzy. Joel shouted from behind him, "Rosa, I found your poster! Too bad, though—Max found it first!" Rosa ran outside. She stared at her poster. It was torn and covered in Max's drool. At that moment Rosa felt like crying, but instead she began to laugh.

"Ah, Max—you found your favorite thing!"

So Rosa took her poster to school. When she presented it to her class, she said, "My poster shows my favorite things: my family and my dog. But since I couldn't glue my dog to the poster, I glued his old favorite toy, Mr. Fuzzy. Max liked the poster so much he decided to chew it. I hope you like the poster too!"

Story Map

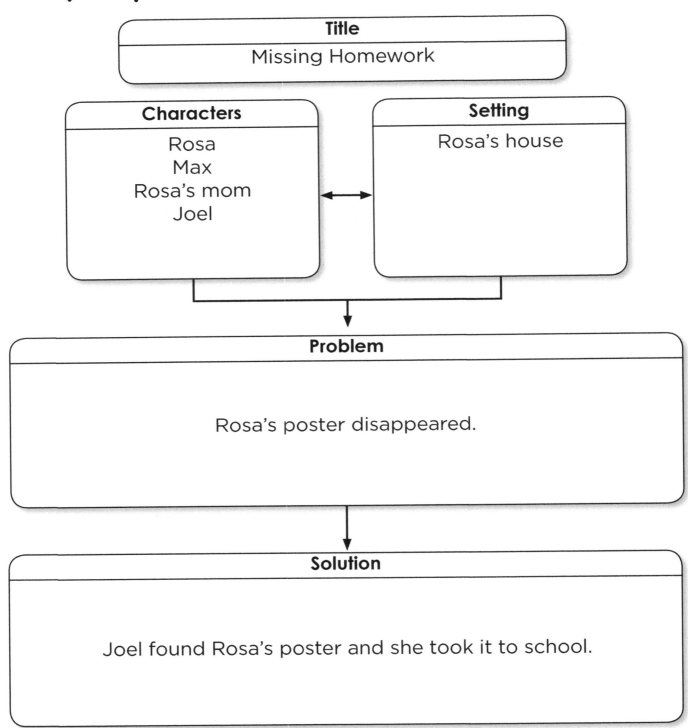

Title

Missing Homework

Characters

Rosa
Max
Rosa's mom
Joel

Setting

Rosa's house

Problem

Rosa's poster disappeared.

Solution

Joel found Rosa's poster and she took it to school.

Name: _____

Dancing the Tinikling

Story Map

Grade 3, Article 1

Written by Jonah Santiago
Illustrated by Micah Graham

Lexile®: 660L, 302 words

"Okay, Angela, are you ready?"

Angela nodded at her sister, Michelle, even though she was a little nervous. Michelle was going to teach Angela how to dance the tinikling. The tinikling was a dance from the Philippines—the country their family was from. Angela's grandparents, parents, and sister had learned the tinikling when they were young.

The family had moved the furniture out of the kitchen so Angela and Michelle would have room. There were two long wooden poles laid side by side on the floor where the table usually was.

"In the Philippines, there are tall birds called tikling birds," Michelle said. "This dance copies the way they step and hop through the tall grass."

Her sister hopped gracefully between the wooden poles. She held out her hand to Angela. "Now you try it. Just copy my movement."

Angela hopped between the poles the way Michelle had. Then Michelle showed Angela some more dance moves. Angela tried to copy her, but she wasn't very good. But Angela was determined.

Angela asked Michelle to practice with her every day after school. Angela even practiced on the playground and while she was walking down the sidewalk!

"You're getting good at this!" Michelle said one day with a smile. "Are you ready to make it harder?"

Angela thought the dance was hard enough already, but she nodded. Her mom and dad lifted the ends of the wooden poles a few inches off of the ground and clapped them together in a slow rhythm. Michelle showed Angela how to jump over the poles as they were moving.

Name: _____

Angela tripped over the poles three times that afternoon, but she got up right away and tried again. The more she practiced, the better she got. Soon, Angela was almost as good at dancing the tinikling as Michelle!

Name_____

Story Map

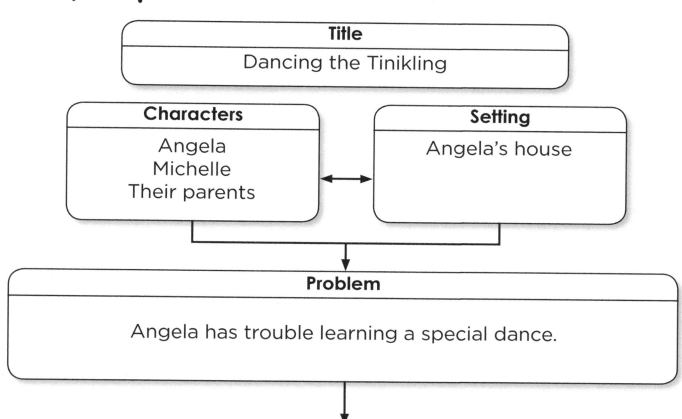

Title

Dancing the Tinikling

Characters

Angela
Michelle
Their parents

Setting

Angela's house

Problem

Angela has trouble learning a special dance.

Plot/Events

1. Angela feels nervous.
2. Her sister teaches her the tinikling dance.
3. Angela can't do it very well but keeps practicing.
4. Her parents lift the poles even higher.

Solution

Angela practices until she becomes almost as good as Michelle at the tinikling dance.

Name: _____

Job Swap

Story Map

Grade 3, Article 2

Written by Heather Anders

Illustrated by Jeff Harvey

Lexile®: 660L, 340 words

"It's time to do your chores, Sam!"

I sighed when I heard my mom call to me from the back door. I'd been outside for most of the morning, climbing trees and pretending that I was the ruler of the backyard. I dragged my feet through the autumn leaves on my way back inside.

My brother, Will, was standing by the refrigerator, reading the chore chart that my mom had just put up. I stood next to him to read the chart. Under the usual list of everyday chores, there was one special chore for each of us. Mom called it the big job of the day, and my big job was that I had to help cook dinner.

"Oh, no," Will joked. "Sam, you're horrible at cooking. We're all going to be poisoned!"

"Yeah, you're probably right," I agreed, even though I knew Will was joking. "You remember that time I added too much salt to the mashed potatoes?"

Will wrinkled his nose and stuck his tongue out as if he could taste the potatoes again. Will was great at cooking. "What's your big job today?" I asked him, looking at the chart again.

"Raking the leaves in the yard," he said with a sigh. "My least favorite chore, after mowing the lawn. It's so cold and windy outside."

"Are you kidding me? It's so much better than being stuck inside chopping onions."

Then, an idea came to me. "Hey, do you think Mom would let us switch chores? I'll rake the yard if you help out with dinner."

"That's a great idea!"

Name: _____

We found Mom cleaning the bathtub and asked her if we could switch jobs. She said it was fine, as long as we both thought it was fair and agreed to the trade. Will and I both agreed at the same time.

As soon as I could, I went running back outside into the fresh air. Raking leaves was almost as good as being ruler of the backyard. And it was much better than chopping vegetables!

Name _____

Story Map

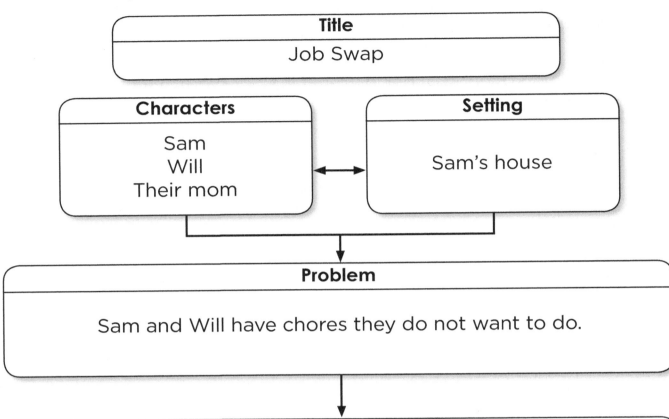

Title

Job Swap

Characters

Sam
Will
Their mom

Setting

Sam's house

Problem

Sam and Will have chores they do not want to do.

Plot/Events

1. Sam doesn't want to cook dinner. _____
2. Will doesn't want to rake leaves. _____
3. They trade jobs so Sam can go back outside. _____
4. _____

Solution

They asked their mother if they could switch chores.

Notes

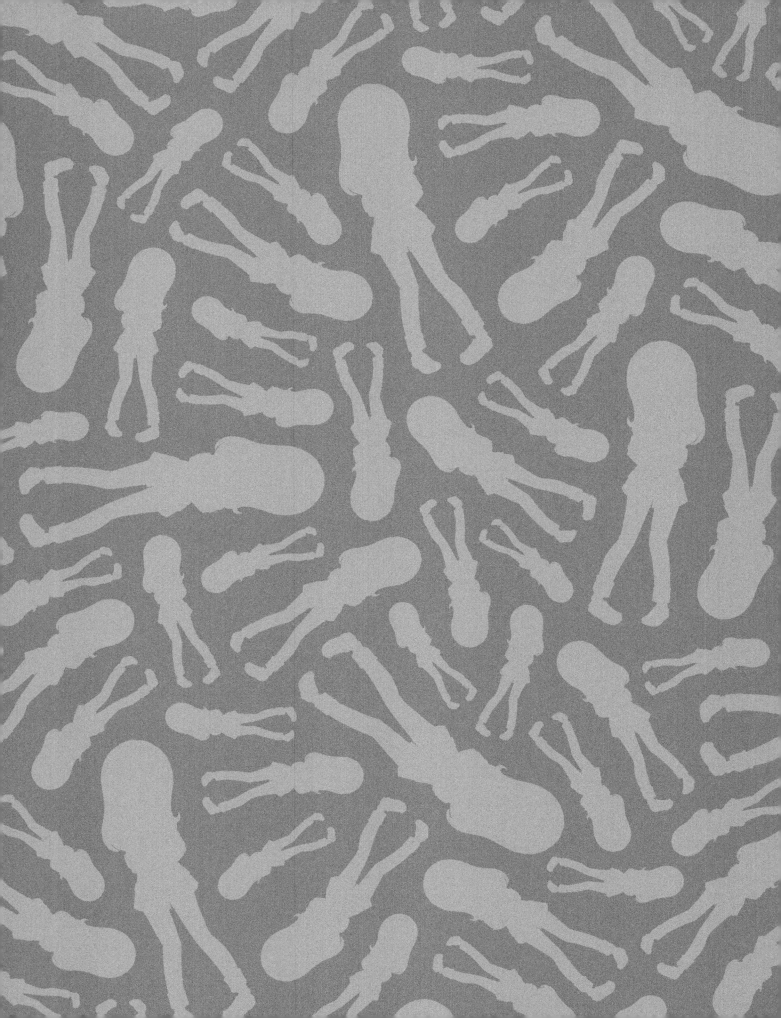

READING COMPREHENSION GRADES 2–3

RETEACHING LESSONS

Developed with research-based methods, these lessons provide engaging activities and print-ready supporting materials to help students review and practice reading comprehension and analysis skills, such as main idea, compare and contrast, and context. Each lesson can be used for small group intervention or adapted for whole-class use.

Analyze data in the Imagine Learning Action Areas Tool to identify groups of students who struggle with reading comprehension and use the Reteaching Lessons to provide additional support.

- Complete lesson plans that include modeling, practice, and assessment
- Lesson format includes sentence starters and frames to aid students in academic language production
- Instruction and reading topics that engage student interest and connect to everyday experiences
- Materials and strategies specifically designed for struggling readers

Progress Tracking Sheet

Date	Student Name	Lesson/Skill	Intervention Successful (Y/N)	Notes

Progress Tracking Sheet

Date	Student Name	Lesson/Skill	Intervention Successful (Y/N)	Notes

Progress Tracking Sheet
Copyright © Imagine Learning, Inc.

Imagine Learning®

Notes

Reteaching Lessons

Cause/Effect

LEARNING OBJECTIVE: Connect causes and effects in an informational text.

LANGUAGE OBJECTIVE: Explain cause and effect relationships orally and in writing using sentence frames for academic language support.

Lesson Overview

Students read an informational text about landforms and identify cause and effect relationships.

Materials

- Printouts of "Landforms" (one per student)
- Printouts of Comprehension Questions (one per student)

Teach and Model: Identifying Cause and Effect Relationships

Tell students they will read a text about landforms and practice answering cause and effect questions about it.

Review the concept of cause and effect. Say: ***When something causes something else to happen, we call it* cause and effect. *The* cause *is why something happened. The* effect *is what happened. For example, "The glass broke because I dropped it." The broken glass is the effect. What is the cause?*** (You dropped it.)

Distribute a copy of "Landforms" to each student. Read aloud the Strategy box on the student printout. Say: ***When we understand how an author organizes his or her writing, we can better understand what we read. Sometimes authors let us know they are writing about a cause and effect by using signal words. What signal words should you look for?*** (*because, since, so,* and the phrase *if . . . then*)

Model how to identify signal words and talk about causes and effects using the sentence frames. Say: ***Listen for a signal word in this sentence. I hurt my arm because I fell down. What was the effect?*** (You hurt your arm.) ***What signal word did I use that can help us find the cause?*** (*because*) ***I hurt my arm because . . .*** (You fell down.) Model using a sentence frame to restate the answer: ***Falling down caused me to hurt my arm.***

Continue modeling with a different signal word: Say: ***Listen for a signal word in this sentence. If I turn on a heater, then the room will get warmer. What signal phrase did I use?*** (*If . . . then*) ***What is the effect of turning on a heater?*** (The room will get warmer.) Model using a sentence frame to restate the answer: ***Right, the effect is the room getting warmer.***

Have students choral read paragraphs 1 and 2 of "Landforms." Say: ***What signal word did you see in paragraph 2?*** (because) ***Circle the signal word. What is the effect of plates pushing together?*** (A big fold in the earth forms. That fold becomes a mountain.) Guide students to annotate their copy of the text. Have them underline the effect and label it *E* for *effect.*

Continue: ***What is the cause of the fold forming?*** (Giant plates push into one another.) Guide students to underline the cause and label it *C* for *cause.*

Practice and Apply: Connecting Causes and Effects

Explain that students will work with a partner to practice finding other causes and effects in the text.

Pair students. Have students follow along as you read paragraph 3 of "Landforms." Then have partners work together to identify the signal word, the cause, and the effect. Encourage them to use the sentence frames in the Strategy box as they discuss the cause and effect with their partner. Remind students to:

- ***Circle the signal word or phrase.*** (If . . . then)
- ***Underline the cause and label it* C.** (The water washes away the earth.)
- ***Underline the effect and label it* E.** (A valley forms.)

 Imagine Learning®

After partners have annotated their texts, lead a group discussion about the cause and effect in paragraph 3. Use these prompts:

- **What signal word or phrase did you circle?**
- **What is the cause?**
- **What is the effect?**

Check Progress

Distribute the Comprehension Questions to each student.

To check individual progress, have each student read paragraph 4 of "Landforms" and answer the questions in writing. Remind students to look for signal words.

1. What is the effect in paragraph 4?

The effect is (a plateau forms.) _____

2. What is the cause in paragraph 4? Complete this sentence to tell about the cause and its effect.

(Possible response: A volcano making hardened layers) causes (a plateau to form.) _____

Check individual responses. If the student's writing shows that he or she can identify and explain cause and effect relationships within a text, consider the intervention successful.

Name _____

Landforms

Strategy: To identify cause and effect, look for the signal words *because, since, so, if . . . then.* Use these sentence frames:

_____ **causes** _____ .

The effect is _____ .

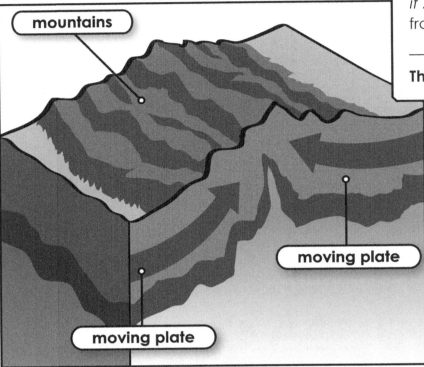

Reteaching Lessons

[1] Earth has many landforms. Mountains, valleys, and plateaus are three kinds of landforms. How are these landforms made?

[2] Giant plates are under Earth's surface. These plates push into one another over time. A big fold in the earth can form. The fold forms because of the plates pushing against one another. The picture above shows how the fold becomes a mountain.

[3] Valleys are low areas of land. They are found between hills. They are also found between mountains. One way a valley forms is from flowing water. Over time, flowing water washes away the earth. If the water washes enough earth away, then a river valley forms.

[4] A plateau is a flat, raised landform. A plateau can be a sign that a volcano erupted long ago. When a volcano erupts, lava flows out. The lava hardens in layers. If the volcano makes enough layers, then a plateau forms.

Landforms
Copyright © Imagine Learning, Inc.

264

Comprehension Questions

Use what you learned in "Landforms" to answer each question.

1. What is the effect in paragraph 4?

The effect is _____

_____

_____

_____

_____

2. What is the cause in paragraph 4? Complete this sentence to tell about the cause and its effect.

_____ causes _____

 Imagine Learning®

Compare and Contrast
Informational Text

Grades 2–3
20 Min.

CCSS.RI.3.9

LEARNING OBJECTIVE: Compare and contrast the most important details from two texts on the same topic.

LANGUAGE OBJECTIVE: Explain similarities and differences orally and in writing using a word bank for academic language support.

Lesson Overview

Students read two informational texts about working dogs and complete a Venn diagram to compare and contrast the texts.

Materials

- Printouts of "Herding Dogs" and "Guide Dogs" (one per student)
- Printouts of Venn Diagram (one per pair of students, plus one for modeling)
- Printouts of Comprehension Questions (one per student)

Teach and Model: Comparing and Contrasting

Tell students they will read two texts about working dogs and tell how the two are alike and different.

Review the concept of comparing: **When you compare two things, you tell how they are alike. For example, you can compare an apple to an orange: an apple and an orange are alike because they both grow on trees.**

Ask: **What is another way an apple and an orange are alike?** (Possible responses: They both are foods; are round; taste sweet; are healthy; can have seeds; are used to make juice.) Confirm correct answers. Say: **When you tell how an apple and an orange are alike, you can use the word** both. **Both taste sweet. Both is a good word to use when comparing two things. Let's create a chart and list other words we can use for comparing.**

Draw a T-chart and label the left column *Compare*. Write the word *both* under *Compare* and say: **Let's think of other words and phrases we can use to tell how two things are alike. For example, you might say, "An apple and an orange are the same because they are fruits." What word did I use to compare?** Write *same* under *Compare* on the T-chart.

Continue guiding students to brainstorm words for comparing as they discuss the similarities between an apple and an orange. Record the words in the chart. Ask: **What other words can we use to compare two things?** If students have difficulty identifying additional words, elicit responses with prompts such as: **You can eat an apple. You can eat an orange, too. What word did I use to compare?** (too)

Add the label *Contrast* to the right column of the T-chart. Review the concept of contrasting: **When you contrast two things, you tell how they are different.** Say: **Apples are crunchy. Are oranges crunchy?** (no) Model a contrasting statement: **An apple and an orange are different because an apple is crunchy and an orange is soft. Different is a good word to use when contrasting two things.** Write *different* under *Contrast* on the T-chart.

Sample Word Bank

Compare	Contrast
both	different
same	but
too	not
also	more/less
alike	

Ask: **What is another way an apple and an orange are different?** (Possible responses: An apple has a thin peel you can eat, an orange has a thick peel you take off; An apple is red, green, or yellow, but an orange is orange; An apple has a smooth skin, but an orange is more bumpy. You cut an apple in slices, but an orange already has sections.)

Continue guiding students to identify words for contrasting as they discuss the differences between an apple and an orange. Record the words in the chart. If students have difficulty identifying additional words, elicit responses with prompts such as: **You can eat the peel of an apple, but you don't usually eat an orange peel. What word did I use to contrast?** (but)

Connect the concept to reading comprehension: **When you read two texts with similar topics, you can compare and contrast information from the two texts.**

Compare and Contrast—Informational Text (Grades 2–3)
Copyright © Imagine Learning, Inc.

Imagine Learning

Distribute "Herding Dogs" and "Guide Dogs" to each student. Say: *I will read the first paragraph of "Herding Dogs" aloud. Listen and follow along as I read.* Read aloud from the first text.

Then say: *Now I will read the first paragraph of "Guide Dogs." Listen for ways that herding dogs and guide dogs are alike or different. When you hear one way they are alike, hold up your thumb. When you hear one way they are different, point your thumb down.* Read aloud from the second text.

Display a Venn Diagram for the group to view and tell students: *Now we will compare and contrast herding dogs and guide dogs. We can use this diagram to show how the dogs are alike and different.*

Have students choral read the first paragraph of each text again. Then ask: *What is one way herding dogs and guide dogs are alike?* (They both work/have jobs.) Have students circle the words *job* and *work* in the first paragraph of each text.

Model how to complete the Venn Diagram: *To tell how herding dogs and guide dogs are the same, I will write words in the middle of the diagram under* Both. *What words did you circle in each text?* Write *job* and *work* in the inner circle of the diagram. Model a comparison statement using a word from the T-chart: *Herding dogs and guide dogs both have jobs.*

Model how to contrast using the Venn Diagram. Say: *Now let's look for ways that herding dogs and guide dogs are different.* Prompt students to read the last sentence in each of the first paragraphs to answer these questions: *What do herding dogs work with?* (other animals) *What do guide dogs work with?* (people) Confirm correct responses and write *other animals* under *Herding Dogs* and *people* under *Guide Dogs* on the diagram.

Model a contrasting statement using a word from the t-chart. Say: *Herding dogs and guide dogs are different because herding dogs work with animals, and a guide dog works with people.*

Practice and Apply: Complete a Venn Diagram

Pair students with a partner and distribute a Venn Diagram to each pair. Tell students they will practice comparing and contrasting using the diagram. Read the instructions on the diagram page aloud before students begin.

Explain: *I will read the two texts aloud while you follow along. One partner will circle words and phrases that tell how a herding dog and a guide dog are alike. The other partner will underline words and phrases that tell how they are different. Then you will work together to compare and contrast the dogs using your Venn Diagram.*

Read both texts aloud. Then have partners compare details from their annotated texts, rereading together when necessary. After partners have annotated their texts, have them complete their Venn Diagram. Tell students to practice using the words from the T-chart you created at the start of the lesson as they help each other complete the Venn Diagram. Responses may vary. The example below shows possible responses.

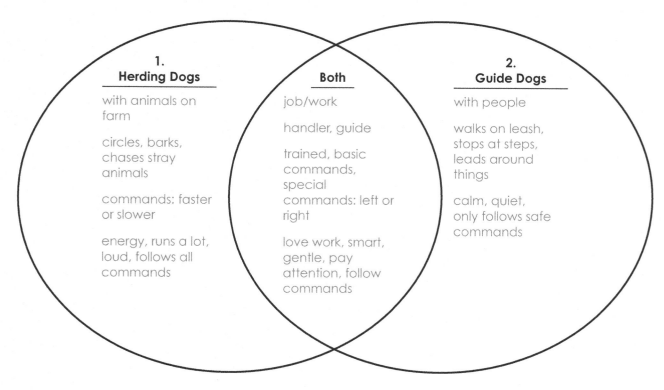

Check Progress

Distribute the Comprehension Questions to each student. Read aloud the directions and the questions before students begin.

1. What is one way that a herding dog and a guide dog are alike?

   A herding dog and a guide dog are alike because both <u>(Possible responses: have a job; work with a handler; are</u> <u>trained to follow basic and special commands; love to work; are smart and gentle; pay attention.)</u>

2. What is one way a herding dog and a guide dog are different?

   A herding dog and a guide dog are different because <u>(Possible responses: a herding dog runs, barks, and chases</u> <u>animals, but a guide dog walks, stays quiet, and guides a person.)</u>

Check individual responses. If the student can answer both questions correctly, consider the intervention successful.

Reteaching Lessons

Herding Dogs

[1] Most people know that dogs make good pets. Some dogs are good workers, too. Herding dogs have a big job. They work with other animals on farms.

[2] A herding dog works with a handler. It helps that person herd animals. A herding dog guides sheep, goats, and cows. If the herd goes the wrong way, the dog circles around and barks. Sometimes an animal wanders away. The dog goes after it and chases the stray animal back to the herd.

[3] A herding dog is trained for its job. First, it learns simple commands such as **sit** and **come**. Then it learns special commands. It learns when to go left or right, faster or slower. These commands help the dog do its job.

[4] A good herding dog has a lot of energy. It runs a lot! It is smart, gentle, and loves to work. It is loud, but it will not hurt the other animals. A herding dog also pays attention to its handler. It follows every command right away.

[5] Herding dogs have an important job. Training helps them get the job done.

Guide Dogs

[1] Guide dogs have a special job. They help people who cannot see. They live with people and work for them.

[2] A guide dog works with a person who is blind. That person is their handler. A guide dog walks on a special leash. It guides its handler from place to place. When the dog reaches steps, it stops. The handler knows then to step up or down. A guide dog also leads its handler around things in their path.

[3] A guide dog gets a lot of training. Just like other dogs, it learns commands such as **down, sit, stay**, and **come**. A guide dog also learns to go left or right on command.

[4] Guide dogs love to work. Dogs that are smart, calm, and quiet make the best guide dogs. They walk at the same speed as their handler. They also pay attention at all times. Good guide dogs follow commands. But they know when NOT to follow a command, too. They only follow a command if it is safe to do so.

[5] Guide dogs are trained to help. They make a big difference in people's lives.

Venn Diagram

Use what you have learned in the two texts to compare and contrast herding dogs and guide dogs. In circle 1, write details about herding dogs. In circle 2, write details about guide dogs. Write words in the middle that tell how the dogs are alike.

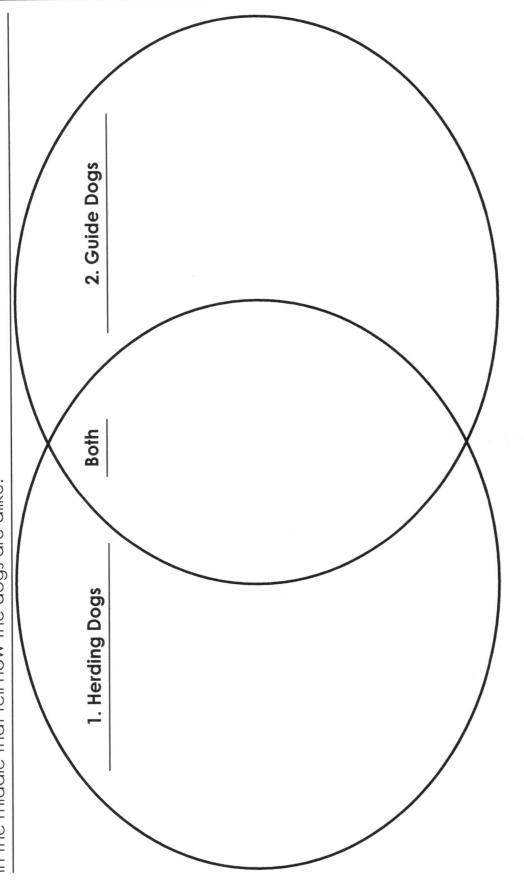

1. Herding Dogs

Both

2. Guide Dogs

Venn Diagram: Herding Dogs and Guide Dogs

Imagine Learning®

Comprehension Questions

Use the Venn Diagram you completed for "Herding Dogs" and "Guide Dogs" to answer each question.

1. What is one way that a herding dog and a guide dog are alike?

   A herding dog and a guide dog are alike because both _____

   _____

   _____

   _____

   _____

2. What is one way a herding dog and a guide dog are different?

   A herding dog and a guide dog are different because _____

   _____

   _____

   _____

   _____

   _____

Reteaching Lessons

 **ImagineLearning**

Comprehension Questions: Herding Dogs and Guide Dogs

Compare and Contrast

Literature

Grades 2–3

25 Min.

CCSS.RL.2.9
TEKS 110.13.6.B

LEARNING OBJECTIVE: Compare and contrast two versions of a similar story.

LANGUAGE OBJECTIVE: Explain similarities and differences orally using a word bank for academic language support.

Lesson Overview

Students read two folktales, take notes in Story Maps, and compare and contrast the folktales using a Venn diagram.

Materials

- Printouts of "Red Visits Her Grandmother" (one per student)
- Printouts of "Snow Girl in the Woods" (one per student)
- Printouts of Story Map (two for modeling)
- Printouts of Venn Diagram (one per student pair, plus one for modeling)

Teach and Model: Comparing and Contrasting

Tell students they will read two stories and discuss the ways the stories are alike and different.

Review the concept of comparing: **When you compare two things, you tell how they are alike. For example, you can compare a dog and a hamster: both make good pets.**

Ask: **What is another way a dog and a hamster are alike?** (Possible responses: Both are animals; have fur; like to run.) Confirm correct answers. Say: **When you tell how the dog and the hamster are alike, you can use the word both. Both are animals. Both is a good word to use when comparing two things. Let's create a chart and list other words and phrases we can use for comparing.**

Draw a T-chart and label the left column *Compare*. Write the word *both* under *Compare* and say: **Let's think of other words and phrases we can use to tell how the dog and hamster are alike. For example, you might say, "A dog and a hamster are the same because they are animals." What word did I use to compare?** (same) Write *same* under *Compare* on the T-chart.

Guide students to brainstorm words for comparing: **What other words can we use to compare?** Write the words in the T-chart. If students have difficulty identifying additional words for comparing, prompt them with examples such as: **A dog has fur. A hamster also has fur. What word did I use to compare?** (also)

On the T-chart, label the right column *Contrast*. Review the concept of contrasting: **When you contrast two things, you tell how they are different.** Ask: **Do a dog and a hamster make the same sound?** (no) Model a contrasting statement: **A dog and a hamster are different because a dog barks and a hamster squeaks. Different is a good word to use when contrasting two things.** Write the phrase on the chart.

Ask: **What is another way a dog and a hamster are different?** (Possible responses: A dog goes outside, but a hamster stays in a cage; a dog walks with a leash, but a hamster runs in a wheel; a dog eats meat, but a hamster does not). Continue guiding students to identify words for contrasting as they discuss the differences between a dog and a hamster. Record the words in the chart.

Sample Word Bank

Compare	Contrast
both	different
same	but
alike	not
also	
too	

If students have difficulty, prompt them with examples, such as: **A dog walks with a leash. Does a hamster walk with a leash?**

Connect the concept to reading comprehension: **We can compare and contrast stories by thinking about how the characters, settings, problems, and solutions in two stories are the same and different.**

Display a Story Map. Say: **We will read two stories together and use this Story Map to record information about each story.**

Compare and Contrast—Literature (Grades 2–3)

Distribute "Red Visits Her Grandmother" and "Snow Girl in the Woods" to each student. Read aloud "Red Visits Her Grandmother" and ask the students to follow along.

Guide the group to complete a Story Map for "Red Visits Her Grandmother." Ask the following questions and record the answers in the Story Map:

What are the story's settings, or in what places does the story happen? (in the woods, Grandmother's cottage)

Who are the characters? (Red, Red's grandmother, the wolf)

What is the main character's problem? (The wolf followed Red to her grandmother's house.)

What is the solution? (They trap the wolf and send him far away.)

Have students choral read "Snow Girl in the Woods" with you. Use the same questions to guide the group to complete a second Story Map for "Snow Girl in the Woods."

Settings: in the woods, family cottage

Characters: Snow Girl, Sasha, parents, bear, wolf, fox

Problem: Snow Girl is lost in the woods.

Solution: Snow Girl's dog Sasha rescues her.

Display a copy of the Venn Diagram for the group to view and model comparing the characters. Say: **The characters are similar in the two stories. They are both little girls.** Write *little girls* in the inner circle of the diagram.

Continue: **The characters in two stories are also different. In the first story, the girl is called Red. In the second story, the girl is named Snow Girl.** Write *Red* in circle 1, and *Snow Girl* in circle 2.

Practice and Apply: Compare and Contrast Stories

Explain that pairs will use the Story Maps and their own Venn Diagram to talk about more details that are alike and different, comparing and contrasting the two stories. Pair students with a partner and distribute a copy of the Venn Diagram to each pair.

Read the instructions aloud before students begin. Tell students to practice using the words from the T-chart you created at the start of the lesson as they help each other complete the Venn Diagram. Responses may vary. The example below shows possible responses.

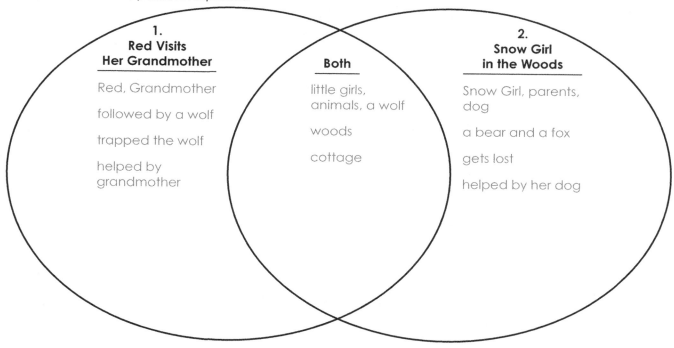

1.
**Red Visits
Her Grandmother**

Red, Grandmother

followed by a wolf

trapped the wolf

helped by
grandmother

Both

little girls,
animals, a wolf

woods

cottage

2.
**Snow Girl
in the Woods**

Snow Girl, parents,
dog

a bear and a fox

gets lost

helped by her dog

Check Progress

To check individual progress, call on each student to answer the following questions orally using the language from the T-chart:

What is one way the two stories are alike? (Possible response: Both stories tell about a girl who is in the woods.)

What is one way the two stories are different? (Possible response: They are different because in one story a wolf follows the girl. In the other story, a wolf, bear, and fox scare the girl.)

Check individual responses. If the student can answer both questions correctly, consider the intervention successful.

Reteaching Lessons

Name _____

Red Visits Her Grandmother
adapted from a European tale

[1] Once there lived a young girl called Red. One day Red went to see Grandmother, who lived on the other side of the woods. Her mother asked her to take a basket of muffins.

[2] "Don't stop along your way, Red," said her mother. "Grandmother is waiting for you."

[3] Red began her walk. Soon, a wolf jumped out and asked where she was going.

[4] "I'm going to my grandmother's house," she replied.

[5] "How nice," he said. " Where does she live?" he asked.

[6] "On the other side of the woods in a little cottage," said Red. " I need to keep walking."

[7] So Red kept going and arrived at her grandmother's cottage. But the sneaky wolf followed her. Red's grandmother was watching. She saw the wolf. When Red came in, Grandmother acted like everything was fine. They sat and enjoyed the muffins.

[8] Soon there was a knock at the door. Grandmother knew it was the wolf. To prepare, she had set out a trap on the doormat. Grandmother opened the window.

[9] "Hello, there," she said.

[10] "Hello, Grandmother," said the wolf. "I've come to help with your house repairs."

[11] "Oh, well that is nice," said Grandmother.

[12] Grandma opened the door and the wolf took a step forward, right into the trap!

[13] They put the trapped wolf into a wheelbarrow, and wheeled him to an open area. They let him go and told him, "Never come back!" The wolf was so scared that he ran far away into the mountains. Red and her family were safe for the rest of their days.

Snow Girl in the Woods
adapted from a Russian folktale

[1] Long ago, a man and a woman lived in a small cottage. They had a little girl named Snow Girl and a little dog named Sasha.

[2] Their dog, Sasha, had an important job. He guarded the chickens. Sasha was usually a good watchdog. But one winter day, a tricky fox snuck into the yard. It ate two of the family's precious chickens. Snow Girl's parents were angry. They sent Sasha away.

[3] When spring came, Snow Girl wanted to go pick berries with the older children. Her parents were worried. They didn't want their little girl going into the woods. But Snow Girl pleaded. The older children promised to take care of little Snow Girl. So her parents allowed her go.

[4] In the woods, the older children ran from berry bush to berry bush. They quickly forgot about their young friend. Snow Girl ran after them. But her little legs did not carry her quickly enough. Soon Snow Girl was alone and lost. She climbed a tree and called out, "Hello! Hello!"

[5] Her friends did not answer her call. Instead, a bear came to the bottom of the tree. He looked up at Snow Girl and said, "Come down. I'll help you."

[6] "No, not you," said Snow Girl. She knew he would try to eat her.

[7] Then, a sneaky wolf came to the bottom of the tree. "Let me help you find your way," he said.

[8] "No, not you," said Snow Girl again. And then, a tricky fox came.

[9] "Come with me," the fox said.

[10] Snow Girl ignored him. She was very scared. Suddenly, she heard a familiar sound.

[11] "Wuf! Wuf!" It was her dog, Sasha. Sasha growled. He snapped at the bear, wolf, and fox. They quickly ran away, scattering in all directions.

[12] Snow Girl laughed with relief. She shouted, "Oh Sasha, my old friend!" Snow Girl climbed down from the tree and Sasha led her safely home.

[13] When Snow Girl arrived home with Sasha, her parents wept for joy. They were grateful to Sasha and welcomed him back into the family.

Name_____

Story Map

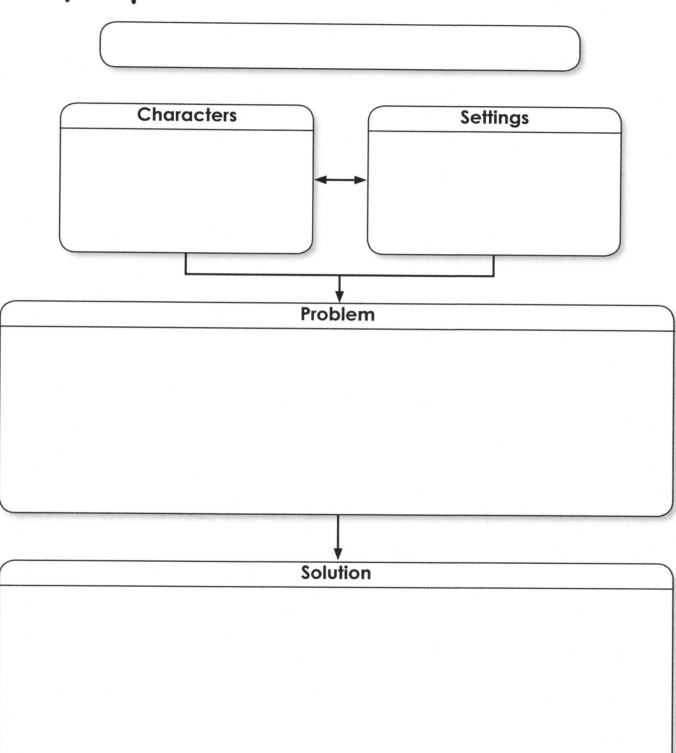

Characters

Settings

Problem

Solution

Venn Diagram

Compare and contrast the stories. Write words and phrases to show how the stories are alike and different. In circle 1, write details from the first story, "Red Visits Her Grandmother." In circle 2, write details from the second story, "Snow Girl in the Woods." Write details in the middle that are alike in the two stories.

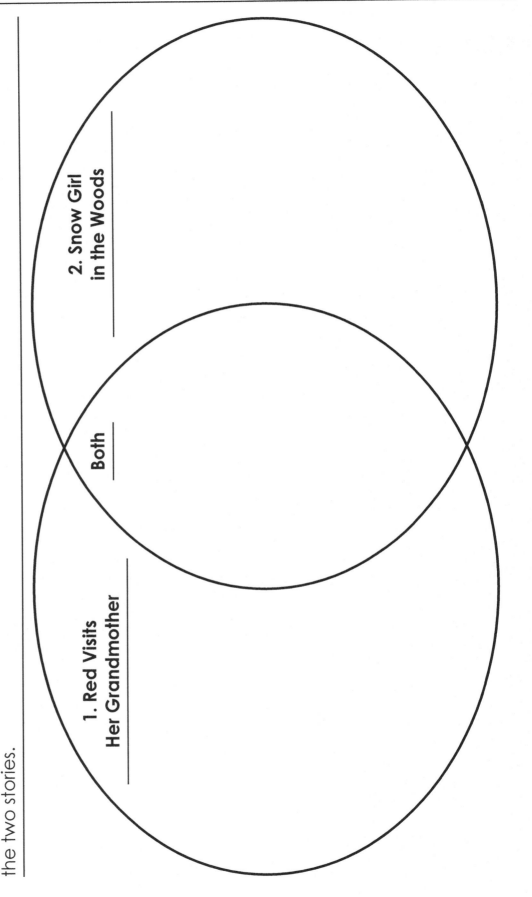

2. Snow Girl in the Woods

Both

1. Red Visits Her Grandmother

Imagine Learning®

Reteaching Lessons

Context

LEARNING OBJECTIVE: Use context clues to determine the meaning of unknown words.

LANGUAGE OBJECTIVE: Explain orally how the meaning of a word is derived from context clues and write a definition of the unknown word.

Lesson Overview

Students read short texts and identify context clues to determine the meaning of unknown words.

Materials

- Printouts of "Word Detectives" (one per student)

Teach and Model: Using Context Clues

Tell students they will practice finding context clues that help them understand the meaning of unfamiliar words.

Review the concept of using context clues. ***When we read we are like detectives; we look for clues to help us understand what we read. The words before and after the word we do not know can be clues. These clues are called* context.**

Distribute "Word Detectives" to each student. Read aloud the directions and choral read the first item.

Model using context clues to determine the meaning of the word *burrow*. Say: ***If I don't know the meaning of the word* burrow, *I can read the sentence again.*** Have students read the first item with a partner and circle words they think are clues. (underground, home) ***The first sentence includes the word* underground. *The last sentence has the word* home *before the word* burrow. *The words* underground *and* home *are context clues. What do you think a burrow is?*** (an underground home for chipmunks)

Practice and Apply: Use Context Clues

Explain that the group will practice using context clues to understand the meanings of the underlined words in the remaining items.

Choral read the sentences in the second item aloud. Ask: ***What is a thistle?*** (a kind of plant) ***What context clues helped you?*** (the words *growing* and *leaves*)

Have pairs of students work together to complete the third item by circling the context clues and writing the definition of *lumber*. When students have finished, call on a volunteer to share the definition and identify the clue words. (*Lumber* means boards cut from trees and used in buildings. Context clues are *woods* and *trees*.)

Check Progress

To check individual progress, have each student complete items 4 and 5 on their own. Tell students to circle the context clues and write the definitions of the underlined words. Meet with individuals to review their answers. If students can identify context clues and write the correct meanings of the words, consider the intervention successful.

4. My dog loves to chase squirrels. She saw one this morning. I had to <u>restrain</u> her to stop her from jumping the fence.

   Restrain means <u>(hold; stop.)</u>

5. Many people choose a <u>profession</u> that helps people. Teachers, doctors, and firefighters all enjoy helping others.

   Profession means <u>(a job.)</u>

Imagine Learning®

Word Detectives

Use context clues to find the meaning of the underlined words and write the definitions.

1. Chipmunks dig a home that is underground. When chipmunks go above ground to gather food, they stuff the food in their cheeks. Then they carry it home to their <u>burrow</u> to eat.

Burrow means _____

_____

2. I found a pretty <u>thistle</u> growing in the yard. When I touched it, its sharp leaves poked my finger.

Thistle means _____

_____

3. Grandfather built his own house in the woods. He cut the <u>lumber</u> from trees on his land.

Lumber means _____

_____

4. My dog loves to chase squirrels. She saw one this morning. I had to <u>restrain</u> her to stop her from jumping the fence.

Restrain means _____

_____

5. Many people choose a <u>profession</u> that helps people. Teachers, doctors, and firefighters all enjoy helping others.

Profession means _____

_____

Word Detectives
Copyright © Imagine Learning, Inc.

Reading Comprehension

Inferential Questions

Grade 2
15 Min.

CCSS.RL.2.1
TEKS 110.13.9

LEARNING OBJECTIVE: Combine evidence from the text and prior knowledge or experience to make inferences about the text.

LANGUAGE OBJECTIVE: Explain answers to inferential questions orally and in writing using sentence frames for academic language support.

Lesson Overview

Students read realistic fiction and answer inferential questions.

Materials

- Printouts of "Surprise at the Dog Park" (one per student)
- Printouts of Comprehension Questions (one per student)

Teach and Model: Answering Inferential Questions

Tell students they will read a story and answer inferential questions.

Review how to make an inference: *When you make inferences, you connect what you see, hear, or read to what you already know. Let's imagine you see a child getting onto a school bus in the morning. We can use what we see plus what we know to make an inference.*

Invite volunteers to respond to each question. Ask: *What did you see?* (a child getting on a bus) *What do you already know about children and buses?* (Some children ride a bus to school each morning.) *So, what is the inference we can make about what we saw?* (The child is taking the bus to school.)

Continue: *So we add the new information we learn to what we already know to make inferences. We do it all the time when we notice things around us. We can also do it when we read.*

Prompt students to explain the first step in answering questions: *When you are answering questions about something you read, what do you do if you don't know the answer?* (Look in the text for the answer.) If necessary, guide students to the answer with gestures of opening a book.

Explain inferential questions: *Sometimes the answer is not right there in the text. So you have to connect what you read and what you know. That is how to answer inferential questions.*

Distribute the story "Surprise at the Dog Park" to each student. Read aloud the information in the Strategy box on the student printout. Then read paragraph 1 of the story aloud and have students point to the words on their paper to track print as you read.

Use the sentence frames to model answering an inferential question: *I wonder, how does Sparky know where they are going? The text says that Jackie and Tom walk to the dog park with Sparky. I already know that people often walk their dogs in the same place. So I think Sparky has been to the dog park before with Jackie and Tom.*

Practice and Apply: Using the Text and Prior Knowledge

Explain that the group will practice answering inferential questions. Ask: *I wonder, how does Sparky feel about going to the dog park?*

Have the group listen for clues as you read aloud the first two sections. Invite students to hold up a finger for each time they hear something that might help answer the question.

After reading the first two paragraphs, call on a volunteer. Say: *Tell about one part of the text that might help us answer the question about how Sparky feels.* If students have difficulty formulating a response in their own words, guide them to use the first sentence frame in the Strategy box. (Possible responses: The text says that Sparky wags his tail; The text says Sparky pulls on his leash; The text says Sparky races across the grass.) Repeat with other students to elicit all three pieces of text evidence.

Guide volunteers to tell about what they already know. Ask: *What do you already know about dogs that can help you answer the question, "How does Sparky feel about going to the dog park?"* (Possible responses: I already know that dogs wag their tails when they are happy; I already know that dogs pull on their leashes when they are excited to go somewhere.)

Reteaching Lessons

Imagine Learning®

Guide volunteers to make inferences based on what the text says and what they already know. (Possible responses: I think Sparky is happy about going to the dog park because he wags his tail; I think Sparky is happy because he pulls on his leash; I think Sparky is happy to go to the dog park because he races across the grass.)

Tell students they will answer questions about the rest of the story. Prompt them to follow along and point to each word as you read aloud.

Check Progress

To check individual progress, distribute the Comprehension Questions to each student.

Remind students to think about what the story says and what they already know to respond to the questions. Read aloud each question. Have students draw in response to each question. Then students may write answers, dictate their answers to a partner, or orally explain their responses to you.

1. Why does someone leave the red book at the park?

(Possible response: Student's drawing shows a person dropping the red book by accident, or shows that a person forgot the book.)

The text says (the man was in the park drawing yesterday.)

I already know that (Possible response: sometimes people forget things or drop things by accident.)

So I think that someone leaves the red book at the park because (Possible responses: he forgot it; he dropped it.)

2. At the end of the story, what do Jackie and Tom hope will happen?

(Possible response: Student's drawing shows Jackie and Tom giving the red book to a man in a blue coat.)

The text says (Possible responses: they have to find that man; Jackie and Tom will make a Lost and Found sign; they want to keep the book safe.)

I already know that (Possible response: people put up a lost and found sign when they are looking for something they lost or for the owner of something they found.)

So I think (Possible response: they hope they will find the owner of the book.)

Check individual responses. If the student's drawing demonstrates understanding, and the student can support the responses orally or in writing, consider the intervention successful.

Reteaching Lessons

Name _____

Surprise at the Dog Park
by Kris Hill

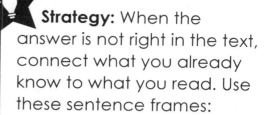

[1] Jackie and Tom walk to the dog park with Sparky.
Sparky wags his tail.
He pulls on the leash.
Sparky knows where they are going.

[2] At the park, Jackie takes off Sparky's leash.
The dog barks and runs across the grass.
Tom laughs and runs after him.

[3] Then Tom stops. "Hey, Jackie!" he yells. "Come over here."
Tom holds up a big red book.
"Somebody left a book here.
It is filled with drawings."

[4] Jackie wants to see it.
"Look! The last picture shows this park," she says.
"The dog in the drawing looks like Sparky."

[5] "Do you remember the man in the blue coat?" asks Tom.
"We saw him yesterday.
He sat on that rock.
He was drawing a picture."

[6] "We have to find that man!" says Jackie.
"We should keep the book safe.
Let's put up a Lost and Found sign, too."

Comprehension Questions

Answer each question about "Surprise at the Dog Park." Draw a picture to show your answer. Then, write your answer. Explain your answer to a partner.

1. Why does someone leave the red book at the park?

The text says _____

_____

I already know that _____

_____

So I think that someone leaves the red book at the park because _____

_____

Comprehension Questions

2. At the end of the story, what do Jackie and Tom hope will happen?

The text says _____

_____

I already know that _____

_____

So I think _____

_____

Reteaching Lessons

Inferential Questions

Grade 3
15 Min.

CCSS.RI.4.1
TEKS 110.15.11

> **LEARNING OBJECTIVE:** Combine evidence from the text and prior knowledge or experience to make inferences about the text.
>
> **LANGUAGE OBJECTIVE:** Explain answers to inferential questions orally and in writing using sentence frames for academic language support.

Lesson Overview

Students read an informational text about desert animals and answer inferential questions.

Materials

- Printouts of "Staying Cool in the Desert" (one per student)
- Printouts of Comprehension Questions (one per student)

Teach and Model: Answering Inferential Questions

Tell students they will read an informational text about desert animals and answer inferential questions.

Review how to make an inference: ***People make inferences all the time. For example, if someone walks into the classroom carrying a wet umbrella, you know that it's raining outside.***

Ask: ***What clue helps you know that it's raining outside?*** (the wet umbrella) ***You already know that people use umbrellas on rainy days. So you add what you see to what you know to make the inference that it's raining outside.***

Continue: ***When answering questions about what you read, sometimes the answer is not in the text. You can answer an inferential question by looking in the text and thinking about what you already know.***

Distribute the text "Staying Cool in the Desert" to each student. Read aloud the Strategy box on the student printout. Then have students choral read paragraph 1 in "Staying Cool in the Desert."

Model using the sentence frames to answer an inferential question: ***Why do few plants grow in the desert? The text doesn't say directly, but it does give a clue. The text says very little rain falls. I already know that water comes from rain, and plants need water in order to grow. So I can infer that few plants grow in the desert because there is not much water.***

Practice and Apply: Using the Text and Prior Knowledge

Explain that the group will practice answering inferential questions. Say: ***The question is, What things do animals need that are hard to find in the desert?***

Have the group listen for clues in the text as you read aloud paragraph 1 again. Invite students to hold up a finger for each clue they hear.

Call on a volunteer to tell about a clue they heard in the text that might help answer this question. If students have difficulty formulating a response in their own words, remind them to use the first sentence frame in the Strategy box. (Possible responses: The text says that few plants grow; The text says that the desert is very hot and animals must stay cool.) Repeat to elicit both pieces of evidence.

Guide volunteers to tell about what they already know. Remind students of the inferential question: ***What things do animals need that are hard to find in the desert?*** Ask: ***What do you already know about what animals need that can help you make an inference with the clues you found in the text?*** (Possible responses: I already know that animals need food and many animals eat plants; I already know that animals need shade and there are not many trees and plants in a desert.)

Guide volunteers to make inferences based on the text clues and what they already know. Ask: ***So what can you infer about what animals need that is hard to find in the desert? Use the clue from the text and what you already know to answer.*** (Possible responses: So I can infer that it is hard for animals to find the food they need in a desert; So I can infer that it's hard for animals to find a place to hide from the hot sun.)

Tell students they will now work in pairs to practice answering another inferential question. Have pairs of students read paragraph 2 of "Staying Cool in the Desert" to answer this question: ***Why is it important for some desert animals to have strong claws?***

Inferential Questions (Grade 3)
Copyright © Imagine Learning, Inc.

 Imagine Learning®

After pairs have read the paragraph and discussed their answers, prompt different volunteers to share using these questions:

- **What does the text say that helps you?** (Possible response: The text says that many desert animals hide underground by digging a burrow.)

- **What do you already know that helps you?** (Possible response: I already know that animals use their claws to dig.)

- **What can you infer based on what the text says and what you already know?** (Possible response: I can infer that it's important for some desert animals to have strong claws so they can hide from the heat during the day.)

Check Progress

Distribute the Comprehension Questions to each student.

To check individual progress, have each student read paragraphs 3–4 of "Staying Cool in the Desert" and answer the questions in writing on the student page. Remind students to return to the text for information clues. Encourage them to use the sentence frames in the Strategy box to write their answers and explain their thinking.

1. How do ground squirrels use their tails for shade?

The text says (ground squirrels have bushy tails.)

I already know that (Possible response: animals stand under something to get shade from the sun.)

So I can infer that ground squirrels use their tails for shade by (Possible response: holding their bushy tails over their bodies.)

2. Why do lizards run quickly in the desert?

(Possible response: The text says lizards run quickly over the hot sand. I already know that hot sand can burn your feet. So I can infer that lizards run quickly in the desert so they don't burn their feet.)

Check individual responses. If the student can correctly answer the questions and support the answers, consider the intervention successful.

Reteaching Lessons

Staying Cool in the Desert

[1] The desert is no easy place to live. Very little rain falls. Few plants grow. During the day, the desert becomes very hot. Yet hundreds of animals live there. How do they stay alive? To live in the desert, animals must stay cool. So they have developed some interesting ways to stay safe in the heat.

Strategy: To answer an inferential question, connect what you already know to what you read in the text. Use these sentence frames:

The text says _____ .

I already know that _____ .

So I can infer _____ .

[2] Many desert animals hide underground to escape the heat. They usually have strong claws. The kangaroo rat is one example. It digs a tunnel, or burrow. It hides there during the day. It comes out at night to hunt for food. Other animals that dig burrows include Gila monsters (HEE-luh MON-sters), iguanas (i-GWAH-nuhs), and desert tortoises. A type of owl also hides underground. But it does not dig much. It lives in burrows made by other animals!

[3] Other desert animals have special bodies that help keep them cool. For example, a desert jackrabbit has huge ears. Its ears help heat escape from its body. Ground squirrels have bushy tails. They use their tails for shade. Long legs can also help. Lizards use their long legs to run quickly over hot sand. Most desert animals are also pale. Light colors take in less heat from the sun.

[4] Desert animals have amazing ways of living where others can't. They escape the heat by hiding from the sun. Their special bodies help keep them alive, too.

Reteaching Lessons

Comprehension Questions

Use what you learned in "Staying Cool in the Desert" to answer each question. Explain how you know the answer.

1. How do ground squirrels use their tails for shade?

The text says _____

I already know that _____

_____

So I can infer that ground squirrels use their tales for shade by _____

_____

_____

_____

2. Why do lizards run quickly in the desert?

_____

_____

_____

_____

_____

_____

_____

_____

Reteaching Lessons

Literal Questions

LEARNING OBJECTIVE: Refer to details in a text to answer literal questions.

LANGUAGE OBJECTIVE: Refer directly to a text to answer literal questions orally and in writing using sentence frames for academic language support.

Lesson Overview

Students read an informational text about archaeologists and answer literal questions.

Materials

- Printouts of "Desert Dig" (one per student, plus one for modeling)
- Printouts of Comprehension Questions (one per student)

Teach and Model: Answering Literal Questions

Tell students they will read a story and practice answering literal questions.

Review the concept of answering literal questions: Hold up two fingers and ask: ***How many fingers am I holding up?*** (two) Say: ***This is an example of a literal question. The answer is right here. All you have to do is look to find the answer.*** You might model with a second example. Hold up a magazine, then ask what the magazine is called. Explain that your question is literal because the answer is right on the cover of the magazine.

Continue: ***Literal questions are questions that have answers right in the text. If you don't remember the answer to a question, you can look in the text.***

Distribute copies of "Desert Dig" to each student. Display a copy that can be viewed by the group.

Read aloud the first sentence in the text: ***"Dr. Hall and Dr. Park are looking for clues in the desert."*** Then say: ***If I pay attention to what the text says, I can more easily answer literal questions. If I forget what the text says, I will look back at the text to find important words.***

Review the Strategy box with students. Show students how to annotate the text by underlining important words that are in questions. Say: ***The question is: "What are Dr. Hall and Dr. Park looking for in the desert?"*** Say: ***I think the words*** **looking for** ***are important words. I'm going to look back at the text to see if I find these words.***

Think aloud and underline *looking for* in the first sentence. Say: ***I found the words in the text. Now I need to answer the question.*** Invite a volunteer to help answer. Confirm the correct answer: ***Dr. Hall and Dr. Park are looking for clues. We found the answer right in the text.***

Read the next two sentences aloud. Then continue modeling how to return to the text to find important words that are also in a question. Say: ***Let's answer another question by paying attention to words in the question and returning to the text. The question is: "What do Dr. Hall and Dr. Park think about this place in the desert?"*** Explain: ***We want to know what Dr. Hall and Dr. Park*** **think.** Guide students to find the word *think*. Invite a volunteer to answer the question using the sentence frame or his or her own words. (The text says they think people might have lived here a long time ago.)

Practice and Apply: Find Details in the Text

Explain that the group will answer more literal questions and mark their text by underling important words.

Read paragraph 2 aloud. Ask: ***What important words are in this question: What do Dr. Hall and Dr. Park use to help them?*** (Possible responses: *use, help*) Say: ***Let's look for*** **use** ***in the text.***

Invite a volunteer to show how he or she found the word *uses* in the passage. Have pairs talk about what the text says. Invite pairs to share answers to the question. (The text says they use a map and special tools.)

Have partners read paragraph 3 and discuss the answer to this question: ***What might Dr. Hall and Dr. Park find?*** Partners should underline an important word (*find*) and discuss their answers. Invite a volunteer to share the answer. (The text says they might find pieces of pottery and bones.)

Reteaching Lessons

Check Progress

Distribute the Comprehension Questions to each student.

To check individual progress, have each student read paragraph 4 of "Desert Dig" and answer the questions in writing on the student page. If a student struggles to write the answers, allow the student to answer orally.

1. Why do Dr. Hall and Dr. Park hold the objects carefully?

The text says they hold the objects carefully because (they are delicate and might break.)

2. How do the items help Dr. Hall and Dr. Park?

(The items help them know more about the people who lived here.)

Check individual responses. If the student can correctly answer the questions and support the answers, consider the intervention successful.

Reteaching Lessons ⌄

Desert Dig

> **Strategy:** To find an answer that is right in the text, look for important words in the question. Then look back in the text for the same words. Use these sentence frames:
>
> **The important words in the question are _____ .**
>
> **The text says _____ .**

[1] Dr. Hall and Dr. Park are looking for clues in the desert. They think people lived here a long time ago. They want to learn about these people.

[2] Dr. Hall and Dr. Park work with a team of scientists. Dr. Park uses a map. This helps him choose a spot to dig. Dr. Hall uses special tools for digging.

[3] They will study the things they find. They might find pieces of pottery. They might find bones.

[4] They hold the objects carefully. The objects are very delicate. They could break. Each item that Dr. Hall and Dr. Park find helps them. The items help them know more about the people who lived here.

Name _____

Comprehension Questions

Read the text "Desert Dig" and answer the questions in complete sentences.

_____

1. Why do Dr. Hall and Dr. Park hold the objects carefully?

The text says they hold the objects carefully because _____

_____

_____

_____

_____

2. How do the items help Dr. Hall and Dr. Park?

_____

_____

_____

_____

_____

Literal Questions

LEARNING OBJECTIVE: Refer to details in a text to answer literal questions.

LANGUAGE OBJECTIVE: Refer directly to a text to answer literal questions orally and in writing using sentence frames for academic language support.

Lesson Overview

Students read an informational text about snow formation and answer literal questions.

Materials

- Printouts of "Snow Report" (one per student)
- Printouts of Comprehension Questions (one per student)

Teach and Model: Answering Literal Questions

Tell students they will read a text and practice answering literal questions using the information in the text.

Review the concept of literal questions. Say: **Let's look at the back corner of the classroom.** Point to a specific spot, such as a bookcase or desk. Continue: **Now, use what you see to answer a question.** Ask: **What is located at that specific spot?** (Possible responses: Students might name furniture, books, posters, or other school materials.) Confirm correct answers.

Connect the concept to reading comprehension: **You named what you saw when you looked in that spot. The answers are right there. When we answer literal questions about a text, we find answers that are right in the text. To answer correctly, you use what the text says.**

Distribute copies of "Snow Report" to each student. Read aloud the Strategy box on the student printout. Read aloud paragraphs 1 and 2 in "Snow Report" and have students choral read.

Model using sentence frames to answer a literal question: **The first literal question is: "When do water droplets turn to ice crystals?" If I don't remember the answer, I can look in the text. The important words in the question are water droplets and ice crystals. I will look for those words in the text.**

Have a volunteer read aloud the first three sentences of the second paragraph again. Say: **The words water droplets and ice crystals are in the text, too. The text says the droplets turn to ice crystals when the temperature of the air of the cloud is near or below freezing. That is the answer.**

Practice and Apply: Find Details in the Text

Explain that the group will practice answering literal questions. Say: **The literal question is: "How do ice crystals form?" The words ice crystals and form are in the question, so let's look in the text for those words.**

Have students choral read the rest of paragraph 2. After reading, return to the text. Tell students to underline the words *ice crystals* and *form*.

Next, prompt a volunteer to answer the question in a complete sentence. Ask: **What are the important words in the question? Use a complete sentence to answer.** (The important words in the question are *ice crystals* and *form*.) If students have difficulty formulating a complete sentence to respond, remind them to use the first sentence frame in the Strategy box.

Continue guiding the student. Ask: **What does the text say that answers the question?** (The text says that ice crystals can form around dust or dirt in the air.)

Tell students they will now work in pairs to practice answering this literal question: **When do snowflakes fall?** Tell students: **First, talk with your partner about what important words are in the question. Then, together, look for the words in the text.**

Allow partners time to discuss the question and find the answer. Then call on one volunteer to tell what important words they looked for. (Possible response: The important words in the question are *snowflakes* and *fall*.)

Call on a different volunteer to answer the question. Ask: **What does the text say that answers the question?** (The text says when the ice crystals get too heavy, they fall as snowflakes.)

Imagine Learning®

Check Progress

Distribute the Comprehension Questions to each student.

To check individual progress, have each student read paragraphs 3–4 of "Snow Report" and answer the questions in writing on the student page. Remind students to look for important words in the question and text. Encourage students to underline or circle the important words.

1. What do all snowflakes have in common?

The text says (all snowflakes have six sides.)

2. What must happen for snowflakes to stay frozen on the ground?

(The text says if the temperature near the ground is cold, the flakes will stay frozen.)

Check individual responses. If the student can correctly answer the questions and support the answers, consider the intervention successful.

Snow Report

[1] You turn on the TV. The weather person reports a chance of snow for later that day. Good news! Maybe there will be enough for a snowball fight with your friends. But, what needs to happen outside for snow to fall?

[2] Both rain and snow begin as water in a cloud. A cloud is made up of tiny drops of water. When the temperature of the air of the cloud is near or below freezing, the droplets of water turn into ice crystals. Usually these ice crystals form around a bit of dust or dirt in the air. The crystals begin very small. They clump together. They get bigger and heavier. When they get too heavy, they fall from the sky as snowflakes.

[3] No two snowflakes are exactly alike. But they all have something in common. All snowflakes have six sides. Ice crystals that form the snowflakes usually have six sides. So, there is only a certain way the crystals can fit together.

[4] If the temperature near the ground is warm, the snowflakes will melt. The snowflakes become rain. However, if the temperature near the ground is cold, the snowflakes will stay frozen. The snow will pile up on the ground. Then you will have the material you need to make snowballs.

Comprehension Questions

Use what you learned in "Snow Report" to answer the questions in complete sentences.
_____

1. What do all snowflakes have in common?

The text says _____

_____

_____

_____

_____

2. What must happen for snowflakes to stay frozen on the ground?

_____

_____

_____

_____

_____

Reteaching Lessons ❮

Main Idea

LEARNING OBJECTIVE: Identify the main idea of an informational text.

LANGUAGE OBJECTIVE: Discuss and explain the main idea of a text orally and in writing using sentence frames for academic language support.

Lesson Overview

Students read informational texts about museums and bees and identify the topic and the main idea in each text.

Materials

- Printouts of "Children's Museums" (one per student)
- Printouts of "The Importance of Bees" (one per student)

Teach and Model: Identify Main Idea

Tell students they will read informational texts and look for the main ideas.

Review main idea: **The main idea is what the author wants you to know. It is the most important idea in the text. To find the main idea, first think about the topic. The topic is what the author is talking about.**

Have students listen for the topic as you say: **Spring is my favorite season. The weather gets warmer in the spring. I like seeing the beautiful flowers bloom. I also love spring because I can play in puddles after the rain.**

Explain: **The topic of a text can usually be stated in one word or a short phrase. Can you tell me in one word what I was talking about?** (spring)

Continue: **After you know the topic of the text, look for words the author uses over and over again. Then think about what the author is saying most about the topic. This is the main idea. When I talked about spring, I used these words and phrases: favorite, I like, and I love. So what do you think the main idea is?** (Possible responses: Spring is your favorite season; You love spring.) Remind students that the main idea is usually stated at the beginning or end of a text.

Connect the concept to reading comprehension: **Identifying the main idea of what we read helps us remember the important information in the text.**

Distribute the article "Children's Museums" to each student. Read aloud the Strategy box and explain: **We can talk about the author's topic and main idea using sentence frames.**

Have students choral read paragraph 1 of "Children's Museums." Model using the sentence frames to identify and talk about the author's topic: **I noticed the phrase children's museum in the title and in the first paragraph.**

Ask: **What kind of museum is the author talking about?** (children's museums) Explain: **This is the topic. The author's topic is children's museums.**

Model finding repeated words: **I noticed that there were two words that were used twice in the first paragraph. What words were used twice?** (learn and play) Have students circle the words.

Practice and Apply: Identify Main Idea

Explain that the group will continue reading the text and practice identifying and discussing the main idea. Choral read paragraph 2 of "Children's Museums." Then say: **You circled the words learn and play in the first paragraph. Which one of those words was used again in the second paragraph?** (learn)

Continue: **What other word is used in the second paragraph that is also in the first paragraph?** (fun) Have students circle the word in each paragraph.

Explain: **The author's topic is children's museums. The author uses the words learn, play, and fun more than once. I think the main idea will use those words, too.**

Tell students they will now work in pairs to continue reading the text and find words that are used more than once. Have pairs read paragraphs 3–6 of "Children's Museums" and circle words the author repeats.

After partners have finished reading and annotating, have them discuss the topic and the important words. Encourage them to use the sentence frames in their discussion. Prompt group discussion with these questions:

Imagine Learning

- ***What is the author's topic?*** (The author's topic is children's museums.)
- ***What is one important word the author uses over and over again? What is another important word the author uses over and over again?*** (Possible responses: The author uses the word *learn/play/fun/kids/children's museum* over and over again.)

Then have partners discuss the main idea. Encourage them to use the third sentence frame in their discussion. Tell them to underline the sentence in the text that best states the main idea.

Prompt a group discussion with this question:

- ***What do you think the main idea is?*** (Possible response: The main idea is that a children's museum is a fun place for kids to learn and play.)

Check Progress

To check individual progress, have each student read "The Importance of Bees" and answer the questions in writing on the student page. If a student struggles to to write the answers, allow him/her to respond to questions orally.

Introduce the new text. Say: **You will read a short text and answer questions about the author's topic and main idea.**

1. What is the author's topic?

The author's topic is (bees.) _____

2. What important words does the author use over and over?

The author uses the words (Possible responses: bees, need, grow, food, pollen, plants.) _____

3. What is the main idea of the text?

The main idea is (Possible response: People need bees to help grow food.) _____

Check individual responses. If the student can correctly answer the questions, consider the intervention successful.

Reteaching Lessons ❯

Children's Museums
by Jada King

Strategy: To find the main idea, look for the most important thing the author wants you to know. Use these sentence frames:

The author's topic is _____ .

The author uses the words _____ .

The main idea is _____ .

[1] Do you like to learn? Do you like to play? You can do both at a children's museum. It is a fun place to learn and play at the same time.

[2] Maybe you like to dig in the dirt. Many children's museums have Dino Digs. Kids dig for real dinosaur bones! This is a fun way to learn about dinosaurs.

[3] Do you like to climb and jump? You can get your body moving in fun ways at a children's museum. The Adventure Science Center in Tennessee has a giant tower. Kids climb and crawl their way to the top. On their way up, they learn about science.

[4] Perhaps you like to build. Many museums let kids test their building skills. The Boston Children's Museum has a construction area. Kids help build a model city there. They learn about roads. They also learn about bridges and tunnels.

[5] What do you know about animals? Some museums have fun ways to learn about animals. A children's museum in Minnesota lets kids try on a turtle shell. They can also dress as ants and explore the ant hill.

[6] Learning is child's play at a children's museum.

Reteaching Lessons

The Importance of Bees

by Nadia Kader

Read "The Importance of Bees." Then answer the questions.

[1] Bees make honey. Many people love this sweet treat. But bees are important for another reason. People need bees to help grow food.

[2] Bees pollinate plants. They take pollen from one plant to another. Plants need pollen to make fruits and flowers. Without seeds from the fruits and flowers, new plants cannot grow. Bees help apples grow. They help nuts grow. They help lemons and grapes grow, too.

[3] We need bees. They help us grow many favorite fruits and vegetables.

1. What is the author's topic?

The author's topic is _____

2. What important words does the author use over and over?

The author uses the words _____

_____

3. What is the main idea of the text?

The main idea is _____

_____

_____

Reteaching Lessons

Main Idea and Supporting Details

LEARNING OBJECTIVE: Connect supporting details to the main idea in a text.

LANGUAGE OBJECTIVE: Describe supporting details orally and in writing using sentence frames for academic language support.

Lesson Overview

Students read an informational text about children's museums and answer comprehension questions to identify supporting details.

Materials

- Printouts of "Children's Museums" (one per student)
- Printouts of Graphic Organizer (one per student, plus one for modeling)

Teach and Model: Identify Main Idea and Supporting Details

Review main idea and supporting details: ***The main idea of a text is what the author wants you to know. It is the most important idea. The supporting details give important information about the main idea.***

Continue: ***Supporting details can be examples and facts.*** Explain how this works using an example of your own or something such as: ***Recently, I read a text about community gardens. The main idea was that small gardens can grow a lot of food. The author showed creative ways to make plants take up less space. The author also taught that tomatoes and lettuce make a lot of food in a small space. These pieces of information were supporting details that helped me understand the main idea.***

Distribute the article "Children's Museum" to each student. Explain: ***As we read, we will identify supporting details that give important information about the main idea.***

Point out the sentence frames in the Strategy box on the student printout. Explain: ***We can talk about the main idea and supporting details using sentence frames.*** Read aloud the sentence frames.

Have students choral read paragraph 1 of "Children's Museums." Model using the first sentence frame to identify the main idea. Say: ***The main idea is that a children's museum is a fun place to learn and play.*** Have students draw a box around the main idea (the last sentence in the first paragraph of their texts).

Display a copy of the Graphic Organizer. Explain: ***Now that I know the main idea, I will look for facts and examples that give important information about the main idea.***

Have students choral read paragraph 2. Model how to identify supporting details: ***The first sentence says, "Maybe you like to dig in the dirt." Is this sentence talking about children's museums?*** (no) **This is not important information about children's museums.**

Continue: ***Let's try the next sentence. "Many children's museums have Dino Digs." Is this important information about children's museums?*** (yes) ***Does this fact support the main idea that a children's museum is a fun place to learn and play?*** (yes) Write this sentence in the first detail box in the Graphic Organizer.

Practice and Apply: Identify Supporting Details

Distribute copies of the Graphic Organizer to students. Point out the Main Idea box and the sentence within. Guide students to copy the first supporting detail from the Graphic Organizer on display.

Explain that the group will continue to read paragraphs 3–6 and then discuss supporting details. Say: ***Listen for facts and examples that give important information about the main idea. Underline supporting details.***

Read aloud paragraph 3 as students follow along. Encourage them to underline supporting details as you read.

Call on a volunteer and ask: ***What is a fact or example in paragraph 3 that supports the main idea?*** (Possible response: One museum has a giant tower that kids can climb.) Have students write the supporting detail in the first detail box of the Graphic Organizer.

Check Progress

To check individual progress, have each student read paragraphs 4–6 of "Children's Museums" and complete their Graphic Organizers. If students struggle to write the answers, allow them to respond to questions orally.

1. Detail from paragraph 4: <u>(Possible response: Many museums let kids test their building skills.)</u>

2. Detail from paragraph 5: <u>(Possible Response: Some museums have fun ways to learn about animals.)</u>

Check individual responses. If the student can correctly fill in his or her Graphic Organizer, consider the intervention successful.

Reteaching Lessons

Children's Museums
by Jada King

[1] Do you like to learn? Do you like to play? You can do both at a children's museum. It is a fun place to learn and play at the same time.

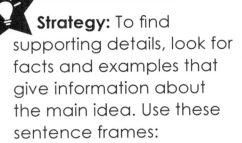

Strategy: To find supporting details, look for facts and examples that give information about the main idea. Use these sentence frames:

The main idea is _____ .

One detail that supports the main idea is _____ .

[2] Maybe you like to dig in the dirt. Many children's museums have Dino Digs. Kids dig for real dinosaur bones! This is a fun way to learn about dinosaurs.

[3] Do you like to climb and jump? You can get your body moving in fun ways at a children's museum. The Adventure Science Center in Tennessee has a giant tower. Kids climb and crawl their way to the top. On their way up, they learn about science.

[4] Perhaps you like to build. Many museums let kids test their building skills. The Boston Children's Museum has a construction area. Kids help build a model city there. They learn about roads. They also learn about bridges and tunnels.

[5] What do you know about animals? Some museums have fun ways to learn about animals. A children's museum in Minnesota lets kids try on a turtle shell. They can also dress as ants and explore the ant hill.

[6] Learning is child's play at a children's museum.

Name _____

Main Idea

A children's museum is a fun place to learn and play.

Detail

Detail

Detail

Main Idea and Supporting Details: Graphic Organizer

Points and Reasons

LEARNING OBJECTIVE: Identify the author's points and supporting reasons in an informational text.

LANGUAGE OBJECTIVE: Discuss the author's points and supporting reasons orally and in writing.

Lesson Overview

Students read an informational text about community helpers and identify the author's points and supporting reasons.

Materials

- Printouts of "Community Helpers" (one per student)
- Printouts of Comprehension Questions (one per student)

Teach and Model: Identifying Author's Points and Supporting Reasons

Tell students they will read an informational text about important helpers in the community and practice finding the author's points and the reasons that support the points.

Review points and supporting reasons: ***Sometimes we want to make an important point. For example, I think that hamsters are the best pets. What is my point?*** (Hamsters are the best pets.)

Continue: ***If I want you to agree with my point or understand it, I need good reasons to support my point. Good reasons will answer the question "Why are hamsters the best pets?" So one reason for my point about hamsters could be that hamsters are soft and cute. It's also fun to watch hamsters run on their wheel.*** Ask: ***Do my reasons answer why I think hamsters are the best pets?*** (yes) Ask a volunteer to think of another reason that answers the question "Why are hamsters the best pets?"

Divide the students into two groups. Tell the groups they will each represent an animal. They will need to think of good reasons to convince you that their animal is the best pet. Ask one group to brainstorm three reasons why fish make the best pets and the other group to brainstorm three reasons why birds make the best pets. After students have had time to discuss, ask them to share their reasons. Then, have students discuss which reason best supported each group's point.

Distribute copies of "Community Helpers" to each student. Then read aloud the title, author's name, and paragraph 1 as students track the print. After reading, say: ***This is a text about different kinds of community helpers. The author, Carla Cruz, wrote that community helpers are important people.***

Say: ***We will look for reasons that support the author's point.*** Read aloud paragraph 2 as students follow along. Model how to identify points and reasons: ***The author makes a point in the first sentence of this paragraph. The point is that ambulance technicians are important community helpers.*** Have students circle the point in paragraph 2.

Continue: ***One reason ambulance technicians are important community helpers is that they arrive quickly in an emergency.*** Have students underline that reason. Then prompt students to identify the remaining two reasons and underline them. (They help us when we are hurt. They teach us how to stay safe when we play or ride bikes.)

Practice and Apply: Identifying Supporting Reasons

Explain that students will practice finding other points and supporting reasons.

Read paragraph 3 aloud as students annotate their texts. Have them circle the point and underline the reasons.

Invite volunteers to answer these questions. Ask: ***What is the author's point in this paragraph?*** (The point is that firefighters are important community helpers.) ***Did the author support her point with reasons?*** (yes) ***What is a supporting reason in the paragraph?*** (Possible responses: They put out fires; they teach us about fire safety; they rescue people from fires; they also rescue animals.) Continue to elicit all four reasons.

Check Progress

To check individual progress, have each student read paragraphs 4–5 of "Community Helpers" and answer the questions in writing on the student page. Read each question aloud for students. If students struggle to write the answers, allow them to answer questions orally.

1. What is the author's point in paragraph 4?

The author's point is <u>(that custodians are important community helpers.)</u>

2. What is one supporting reason?

<u>(Possible responses: They help us keep everything clean and neat; they fix things and make sure the school is a safe place for students.)</u>

Check individual responses. If the student can correctly answer the questions, consider the intervention successful.

Reteaching Lessons

Community Helpers by Carla Cruz

[1] In our community there are many important people that help us every day. Community helpers serve others, and they try to keep people safe and healthy.

[2] Ambulance technicians are important community helpers. They are also called EMTs. They arrive quickly in an emergency. They help us when we are hurt. They can even teach us how to stay safe when we play or ride bikes.

[3] Firefighters are important community helpers. They put out fires. They teach us about fire safety. They rescue people from fires. They also rescue animals.

[4] Custodians are important community helpers. Many of them work in schools. They help us keep everything clean and neat. They fix things and make sure the school is a safe place for students.

[5] It takes many people working together to serve a community. Who are some of the important helpers in your community?

Community Helpers

Comprehension Questions

Use what you learned in "Community Helpers" to answer each question.

1. What is the author's point in paragraph 4?

The author's point is _____

_____

_____

2. What is one supporting reason?

_____

_____

_____

_____

_____

Points and Reasons

LEARNING OBJECTIVE: Identify the author's point and supporting reasons in an informational text.

LANGUAGE OBJECTIVE: Discuss the author's point and supporting reasons orally and in writing using sentence frames for academic language support.

Lesson Overview

Students read a persuasive text about protecting Eastern box turtles and identify the author's point and supporting reasons.

Materials

- Printouts of "Turtles in Danger" (one per student)
- Printouts of Comprehension Questions (one per student)

Teach and Model: Identifying Author's Point and Supporting Reasons

Tell students they will read an informational text about turtles and practice finding the reasons that support the author's point.

Review the concept of points and supporting reasons: **Sometimes we want to make an important point. For example, I think that guinea pigs are the best pets. What is my point?** (Guinea pigs are the best pets.)

Continue: **If I want you to agree with my point or understand it, I need to support my point with reasons. Good reasons will answer the question "Why are guinea pigs the best pets?" Guinea pigs are easy to take care of at home. Guinea pigs are friendly. Guinea pigs are smart. Do my reasons answer why I think guinea pigs are the best pets?** (yes)

Distribute copies of "Turtles in Danger" to each student. Read aloud the Strategy box, text title, and author's name. Have students choral read paragraph 1.

Model discussing points and reasons: **The author, Lia Yung, is talking about keeping turtles as pets. She writes that many people keep turtles as pets. While this information is important, it is not the author's point. The point is what the author wants us to agree with. What do you think the author's point is?** (Wild turtles should be left alone.) Have students circle the author's point.

Read aloud paragraph 2 as students follow along. Then model how to identify reasons that support the author's point: **Why should wild turtles be left alone? The answer to this question will be the reasons that support the point. What reason does paragraph 2 give?** (Possible responses: Eastern box turtles are disappearing; each turtle taken from the wild makes the problem worse.) Prompt discussion: **Do you agree that this is a good reason? Does it help you understand why the author thinks wild turtles should be left alone?**

Practice and Apply: Identifying Supporting Reasons

Explain that the group will practice finding more reasons that support the author's point.

Have students choral read paragraph 3. Then assign students to work with a partner. Have students turn to their partners and talk about the supporting reason in the paragraph. Then prompt group discussion: **What reason does the author give in paragraph 3?** (Possible responses: Wild turtles do better on their own; a turtle doesn't live as long when kept as a pet.)

Imagine Learning®

Check Progress

Distribute the Comprehension Questions. To check individual progress, have each student independently read paragraphs 4–6 of "Turtles in Danger" and answer the questions in writing on the student page.

1. What is a reason in paragraph 4 that supports the author's point?

One supporting reason is (Possible response: that people get bored with wild turtles after they take them home. They set them free in the wild, which makes other turtles sick.)

2. What is a supporting reason in paragraph 5?

One supporting reason is (Possible response: that Turtles are easily frightened and get scared away from their nests when people touch them.)

Check individual responses. If the student can correctly answer the questions, consider the intervention successful.

Reteaching Lessons

Name _____

Turtles in Danger by Lia Yung

Strategy: Look for ways the author makes a point and uses reasons to support it. Use these sentence frames:

The author's point is _____ .

One supporting reason is _____ .

[1] Many people keep turtles as pets. One popular pet is the Eastern box turtle. Sometimes people find them outside and want to keep them. They might also want to play with the turtles. But wild turtles should be left alone.

[2] Every year, there are fewer and fewer Eastern box turtles. Some scientists are troubled by this. They believe these turtles may be in danger. The turtles might soon start disappearing. Each turtle taken from the wild makes the problem worse.

[3] Pet turtles are fun, but wild turtles do better on their own. A wild turtle can live up to 100 years. It doesn't live as long when kept as a pet.

[4] People often get bored with turtles after they take them home. Sometimes they put them back in the wild. This does more harm than good. Pet turtles will usually not survive when set free. They can also pass germs to wild turtles and make them sick. This hurts Eastern box turtles even more.

[5] Sometimes kids just want to play with turtles they find. But wild turtles are easily frightened. They get scared when people touch them. Sometimes mother turtles are scared away from their nests. They become too afraid to lay eggs.

[6] It is hard to stay away from a wild box turtle. They are amazing creatures and fun to play with. But it's best to leave them alone.

Comprehension Questions

Use what you learned in "Turtles in Danger" to answer each question.

1. What is a reason in paragraph 4 that supports the author's point?

   One supporting reason is _____

   _____

   _____

   _____

   _____

2. What is a supporting reason in paragraph 5?

   One supporting reason is _____

   _____

   _____

   _____

   _____

Reteaching Lessons ∨

Story Lesson

LEARNING OBJECTIVE: Determine the lesson in a fable or folktale.

LANGUAGE OBJECTIVE: Discuss and explain the lesson in a fable or folktale orally and in writing.

Lesson Overview

Students read three fables and discuss the story lesson in each text.

Materials

- Printouts of "The Sack" (one per student)
- Printouts of "The Traveler and the Nut Tree" (one per student)
- Printouts of "The Monkey and the Pea" (one per student)
- Printouts of Comprehension Questions (one per student)

Teach and Model: Determining the Story Lesson

Tell students they will read three fables and discuss the lesson in each text.

Remind students: ***Folktales and fables are stories that were made up a long time ago. They are stories that come from cultures all over the world. In fables, the characters often learn a lesson.***

Give a student-friendly definition of *lesson* in context: ***A story's lesson often has to do with how to act and be together with others. The lesson might be to share, to work hard, or to be kind.***

Distribute "The Sack" and read aloud the information in the Strategy box. Then invite students to track the print as you read. Say: ***Follow along as I read aloud. Listen for who the characters are and what is happening.***

Read aloud "The Sack." Model determining the story lesson by discussing the answers to the questions in the Strategy box. Say: ***To understand the story's lesson, I think about who the characters are and what they are like. Who are the characters?*** (Mula and the man with the sack) ***In the beginning of the story, what is the man with the sack like? How does he feel? What does he think?*** (Possible responses: He feels sad; he moans, complains, and cries; he thinks he has very little.) ***I know Mula is clever because he takes the man's sack and tricks him into thinking the sack is lost forever.***

Continue modeling: ***Next I think about the question, "What lesson does one of the characters learn in the story?" To answer this question, it's often helpful to think about which characters change in the story and how they change. In "The Sack," which of the two characters changes?*** (the man with the sack) ***How does he change?*** (He is happy; he no longer moans, complains, or cries.) ***What lesson does the man with the sack learn?*** (He learns to be happy with what he has.)

Practice and Apply: Discussing the Story Lesson

Explain that students will read another fable and then discuss the story lesson with a partner.

Distribute "The Traveler and the Nut Tree" and guide students to read it. Students might choral read, take turns reading a paragraph aloud, or follow along as you read the text aloud.

After reading, have partners discuss the story's character and the lesson the main character learns. Remind them to think about how the main character changes in the end. After partners have discussed the story and the story's lesson, prompt group discussion with these questions:

- ***Who is the character in the story?*** (the traveler)
- ***What is the traveler like in the beginning?*** (Possible responses: He thinks nature is foolish and he would have made the world differently; he thinks he is smarter than nature.)
- ***How does the traveler change in the end?*** (Possible responses: He is glad nature didn't make pumpkins grow on trees; He realizes he isn't smarter than nature.)
- ***What does the traveler learn?*** (He learns that nature knows best.)

Reteaching Lessons

Check Progress

Distribute "The Monkey and the Pea" and the Comprehension Questions to each student. To check individual progress, read the story aloud as students follow along. Then have students answer the Comprehension Questions. If students struggle to to write the answers, allow them to answer questions orally.

1. Who are the characters?

The characters are (the king, Adib, and the monkey.)

2. What is the king like in the beginning?

(Possible response: The king is greedy and wants more land.)

3. What lesson does the king learn in the end?

(Possible response: The king learns not to take too much; he learns not to be greedy.)

Check individual responses. If the student can correctly answer the questions, consider the intervention successful.

Reteaching Lessons

The Sack a tale from the Middle East

[1] One day Mula was going to town. He came upon a man walking down the road. The man was moaning and complaining. "What's wrong?" Mula asked.

[2] The man held up a ragged sack. "All I have in the world is in this sack," the man cried.

[3] "That's too bad," said Mula. Suddenly, he grabbed the sack from the man's hands and ran away.

[4] Mula ran on ahead and then stopped. He put the sack in the middle of the road where he knew the man would find it. Then he hid in the bushes to watch.

[5] The man came down the road, crying. Everything he had was gone. His life was worse than before.

[6] When the man saw his sack in the road, he laughed. "My sack! I thought I'd lost you!" he shouted with joy. He took his sack and walked happily down the road.

[7] Mula watched the man and smiled. "Now he is happy with what little he has!"

Reteaching Lessons

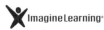

The Traveler and the Nut Tree a tale from India

[1] One day a traveler saw a nut tree. He stopped to rest in its shade. As he rested, he noticed a pumpkin nearby. The huge pumpkin was growing on a thin vine.

[2] He shook his head. "Nature is so foolish," he said. "This big, strong tree should hold the huge pumpkin. The thin vine should hold the tiny nuts. That's how I would have made the world!"

[3] Just then, a small nut fell from high in the tree. It hit the man right on top of his head. Rubbing his head, he thought, "I'm glad that wasn't a pumpkin that fell. It would have flattened me! I learned nature really does know best."

Reteaching Lessons ⌄

Name _____

The Monkey and the Pea a tale from India

[1] A long time ago, a rich king wanted more land. He decided he would take land from a nearby kingdom. The rich king set out on his horse. His helper, Adib, went with him. The king's army marched on foot behind them.

[2] "I must stop to feed the horses," Adib told the king. He gave the horses a bag of tasty green peas. Suddenly, a monkey dropped down from a tree. It grabbed a handful of peas. Then it raced back up the tree.

[3] But the monkey's hand was too full. It dropped a pea. The monkey reached out to catch the falling pea. All the peas fell from the monkey's hand to the ground. The horses quickly ate the fallen peas.

[4] The king laughed. "Monkey, you learned a good lesson. You should have been happy with what you had."

[5] Adib smiled and said, "When you want to take too much, remember the monkey and the pea." The king thought about this. Then he turned around and took his army home.

Imagine Learning

Comprehension Questions

Read "The Monkey and the Pea." Then answer each question.

1. Who are the characters?

The characters are _____

_____

2. What is the king like in the beginning?

_____

_____

_____

_____

_____

3. What lesson does the king learn in the end?

_____

_____

_____

_____

_____

Comprehension Questions: The Monkey and the Pea
Copyright © Imagine Learning, Inc.

Story Map

LEARNING OBJECTIVE: Use a story map to identify the characters, setting, problem, plot, and solution in a text.

LANGUAGE OBJECTIVE: Identify and discuss the important elements in a story using sentence frames for academic language support.

Lesson Overview

Students read realistic fiction and complete a story map to answer questions about important story elements.

Materials

- Printouts of "The Empty Lot" (one per student)
- Printouts of Story Map (one per student)

Teach and Model: Using a Story Map

Tell students they will read a story and complete a Story Map to tell about the characters, setting, problem, plot, and solution.

Distribute a copy of the Story Map to each student. Explain: ***When you map a story, you look for five things. Let's explore the five boxes in our story map.*** Have students point to elements in the Story Map as you review each element. Prompt discussion with these questions:

- ***What kind of information goes in the Character box?*** (Possible responses: the important people or animals in the story; who the story is about)

- ***In which box do we show where the story takes place?*** (Setting)

- ***All stories have problems. What was a problem in a story you've read?*** (Answers will vary.)

- ***What kind of information goes in the Plot box?*** (Events that tell what the characters do to solve the problem.)

- ***Which box shows how the problem is solved?*** (Solution)

Distribute a copy of "The Empty Lot" to each student. Read aloud the information in the Strategy box on the student printout. Then have students choral read the first paragraph of the story.

Say: ***Let's use our Story Map to talk about the important parts of the story.*** Ask: ***Who are the characters in the story?*** (Marisol and Dante) ***What is the setting?*** (an empty lot in the city) Guide students to record information in their Story Maps.

Practice and Apply: Using a Story Map

Tell students they will work with a partner to discuss other parts of the story. Ask: ***What is the problem in the story?*** Have students discuss the problem with a partner and write the problem in their Story Maps.

After partner discussion, call on a volunteer to identify the problem. (Possible response: Marisol and Dante want to turn the empty lot into a playground, but it's too expensive.)

Explain: ***As we continue reading, we will add to the Story Map.***

Have students choral read paragraphs 2–7. Then have partners discuss information they can add to the Story Map. Say: ***If you read about other characters, add them to your Story Map. In the Plot section, write about the events and what the characters do to solve the problem.*** Remind students that they can use the sentence frames in the Strategy box as they discuss parts of the story.

Prompt group discussion with these questions:

- ***What other character did you add to your Story Map?*** (their grandfather, Abuelo)

- ***What are some things the characters do to solve the problem?*** (They ask people in the neighborhood for help, they talk to a city planner, they visit their grandfather.)

- ***What possible solution does Abuelo help them come up with?*** (building a soccer field.)

- ***How might this solve the problem?*** (A soccer field won't cost too much.)

Reteaching Lessons

Check Progress

To check progress, have students read paragraphs 8–10 individually and complete their Story Maps with additional details about the plot and the solution. Then use the following activity to assess students.

Meet with students individually to review their completed Story Maps. Prompt students to answer these questions orally:

- ***After they talked about building a soccer field, what did the characters do next?*** (Possible responses: Then they put up flyers and got other people to help; they posted flyers, raised money, and planted grass.)

- ***What is the solution to the problem in the story?*** (They raised money to build a soccer field, which doesn't cost much. They built the soccer field. Families could play and have picnics in the lot.)

Check individual responses. If the student can correctly answer each question, consider the intervention successful.

Reteaching Lessons ∨

The Empty Lot by Alex Perez

[1] Marisol and Dante looked longingly at the empty lot. It would be a great space for a playground. They asked people in the neighborhood for help. Everyone they talked to thought it would be too expensive. They even talked to a city planner. He thought the space would make a fine parking lot.

> **Strategy:** Use your Story Map and these sentence frames to talk about the parts of a story:
>
> **The characters are _____ .**
>
> **The setting is _____ .**
>
> **The problem is _____ .**
>
> **To solve the problem, the characters _____ .**
>
> **The solution to the problem is _____ .**

[2] Marisol and Dante visited their grandfather, Abuelo.

[3] "What does everyone like to do on the weekend?" Abuelo asked. Marisol and Dante didn't understand. Then they looked at what he was watching on TV.

[4] "Soccer!" shouted Marisol.

[5] "What do you mean?" asked Dante.

[6] "Well, you only need grass to play. And maybe some goals," their grandfather replied.

[7] "That might not cost too much," said Marisol. "Then it would be a place for kids to go. There could be a side for little kids and a side for big kids."

[8] Dante, Marisol, and Abuelo posted flyers around the neighborhood. Many people were willing to help. Soon they had enough money to buy what they needed. In the spring, the lot had new grass. Families came to play soccer and have picnics.

[9] "What a great idea, Abuelo," said Dante.

[10] "You two did all the hard work," he replied.

Name _____

Story Map

Use what you learned in "The Empty Lot" to complete the Story Map.

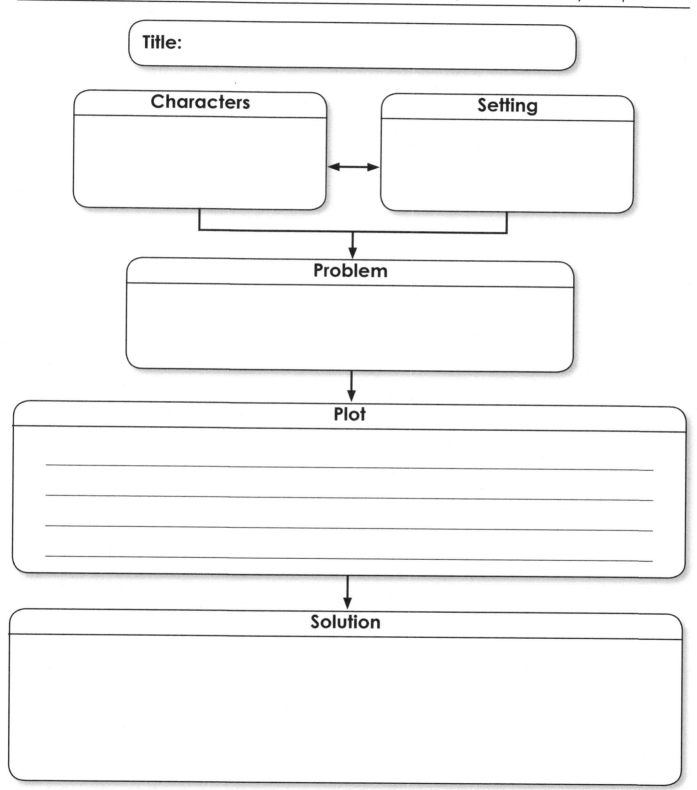

Title:

Characters

Setting

Problem

Plot

Solution

Story Map: Graphic Organizer

Text Evidence

Grade 3

15 Min.

CCSS.RI.3.1
TEKS 110.14.12

LEARNING OBJECTIVE: Cite text evidence to support answers to questions about a text.

LANGUAGE OBJECTIVE: Quote or paraphrase text orally and in writing using sentence frames for academic language support.

Lesson Overview

Students read an informational text about American Red Cross founder Clara Barton and cite text evidence to support answers to questions about the text.

Materials

- Printouts of "Clara Barton" (one per student)
- Printouts of Comprehension Questions (one per student)
- Highlighters

Teach and Model: Citing Text Evidence

Tell students they will first read an informational text about Clara Barton, a woman who helped many people in need, and then they will use information from the text to answer questions.

Connect the meaning of *evidence* to prior knowledge: ***How can you know if a thunderstorm is on its way to your area?*** (Possible responses: I can hear thunder; I see a storm cloud; I hear it on a weather report.)

Continue: ***To know if a thunderstorm is coming, we can look for signs such as the sound of thunder, or dark storm clouds in the sky. These signs are evidence that a thunderstorm is approaching. Evidence supports or proves something is true.***

Connect the meaning of *evidence* to textual evidence. Ask: ***How do you answer a question about something you have read?*** (Look in the text for the answer.)

Continue: ***Sometimes a question about a text might ask you to explain your answer. When you are asked to explain your answer, what should you do?*** (Look at the text for evidence.) ***If you see these sentences in a question, you know you need to cite text evidence:***

- ***Explain your answer.***
- ***Tell how you know.***
- ***Support your answer with details from the text.***

Explain: ***When you are asked to cite text evidence, you go back to the text to find details that support or prove your answer.***

Distribute the text "Clara Barton" to each student. Read aloud the Strategy box on the student printout. Then have students choral read paragraph 1 of the text.

Write this question and read it aloud: ***Why were many men away from home in 1861–1865? Support your answer with details from the text.*** Think aloud and model using the sentence frames to answer the question and cite text evidence: ***The text says that Clara lived during the Civil War. It also says that many of the men were hurt in battles. So I think many men were away from home during the war because they were soldiers fighting in the war.***

Practice and Apply: Citing Text Evidence

Provide students with highlighters. Explain that the group will practice answering questions and citing text evidence.

Write this question and read it aloud. Ask: ***Was Clara Barton brave? Explain your answer.***

Text Evidence (Grade 3)
Copyright © Imagine Learning, Inc.

Have the group listen and highlight text evidence as you read aloud paragraph 2. Prompt a volunteer to answer the question and cite text evidence. (Possible response: I think Clara was brave because the text says she went to the battlefields where hundreds of men were hurt. She went to the place where the army was fighting.)

Tell students they will now work with a partner to answer another question using text evidence. Have partners read paragraph 3 of "Clara Barton" and answer the question: **Why did Clara become known as the "Angel of the Battlefield?" Explain your answer.**

Display the question. Remind students to highlight evidence from the text and discuss their answers with their partner. After pairs have finished discussing, call on volunteers to share their answers and cite text evidence. (Possible response: She became known as the "Angel of the Battlefield" because she helped save lives on the battlefields. The text says the doctor said she arrived just in time. Men were suffering all around him, and he was thankful she came to help.)

Check Progress

Distribute the Comprehension Questions to each student. To check individual progress, have each student read paragraph 4 of "Clara Barton" and answer the questions in writing on the student page. Encourage them to highlight evidence in the text and use the sentence frame in the Strategy box to write their responses in complete sentences.

1. Why do American Red Cross workers travel around the world? Explain your answer.

(Possible response: The workers travel around the world to help people. The text says they go wherever people need help.)

2. Why do people need the American Red Cross to help them find homes? Support your answer with details from the text.

(Possible response: They need the American Red Cross to help them find homes because they lose their homes in disasters. The text says the American Red Cross is there to help after fire or flood, and they rush in after hurricanes and earthquakes.)

Check individual responses. If the student can support the responses with evidence from the text, consider the intervention successful.

Reteaching Lessons

Clara Barton

[1] Clara Barton lived during the Civil War of 1861–1865. Many men were away from home during that time. Clara saw that these men needed help. They needed food, blankets, and clothing. Many were hurt in battles. So Clara looked for ways to help them.

Strategy: To cite text evidence, look for details in the text that support your answer. Use this sentence frame:

The text says _____ .

[2] Clara asked many people to give food, blankets, and clothes. Then she asked leaders to let her follow the army. She wanted to take supplies to the battlefields where hundreds of men were hurt. Clara knew she could help save lives there. In 1862, she was finally given a pass to go where the army was fighting.

[3] One night, Clara appeared at a field hospital near a recent battle. She had a wagon full of supplies. The doctor said she arrived just in time. Men were suffering all around him, and he was thankful that she came to help. Clara became known as the "Angel of the Battlefield."

[4] Clara Barton knew there would always be people who needed help. So she started the American Red Cross in 1881. The American Red Cross still helps people today. American Red Cross workers travel around the world. They find homes for people. They give out water, food, and clothes. After a fire or flood, the American Red Cross is there to help. They rush in after hurricanes and earthquakes, too. They go wherever people need help.

Reteaching Lessons

Comprehension Questions

Use what you read in "Clara Barton" to answer each question. Answer in complete sentences.

1. Why do American Red Cross workers travel around the world? Explain your answer.

   _____

   _____

   _____

   _____

2. Why do people need the American Red Cross to help them find homes? Support your answer with details from the text.

   _____

   _____

   _____

   _____

ImagineLearning®

Reteaching Lessons

Reading Comprehension

Text Features

Grade 2

20 Min.

CCSS.RI.2.5
TEKS 110.13.14.D

LEARNING OBJECTIVE: Use informational text features to find information and understand text meaning.

LANGUAGE OBJECTIVE: Discuss informational text features using a word bank for academic language support.

Lesson Overview

Students interpret and use informational text features to find information.

Materials

- Printouts of "Bubbles, Bubbles, Bubbles" (one per student)
- an informational textbook to model the following text features: **table of contents, title, headings, bold glossary words, images (photographs, charts, maps), captions, glossary, index**
- Printouts of Comprehension Questions (one per student)

Teach and Model: Using Text Features

Tell students they will use text features to find information and answer questions.

Review informational texts and text features: **You already know about different kinds of texts. Some texts called literature tell stories or have poetry.** Ask: **What can you find in informational texts?** (Possible response: facts, true information).

Explain: **Remember that informational texts often have important parts that help you quickly find information.**

Use a familiar informational textbook to point out the important parts of a text as you name and review each one.

- **This is a table of contents. What do you notice about it?** (It's at the beginning of the book; it has page numbers; the information is in a list.) **The table of contents is a list of topics and page numbers to help you know where to go.**

- **This is a title. What do you notice about it?** (It is bigger; it is at the top of the page; it has darker [bold] letters.) **The title tells you what you will be reading about.**

- **These are headings. What do you notice about them?** (They are bold; bigger; at the top of a section.) **Headings go above paragraphs of text. They give you clues about what you will learn in each section.**

- **These are bold words. What do you notice about them?** (The letters are darker/thicker.) **The bold words are important words that can help you understand the topic. You can use the glossary to look up any of the bold words from the book and find their definitions.**

- **These are images. Images can be photographs, charts, or maps. How can they help you as you read an informational text?** (They show us what things look like; they tell where things are found; they give more information.) **Pictures, charts, and maps can give you more information about a topic.**

- **What do you notice underneath the charts and pictures?** (words, sentences, small text) **The words underneath are called captions. Captions explain what you see in the image.**

- **The glossary is usually found at the back of the book. What do you see in the glossary?** (words, definitions, page numbers) **All the bold words from the whole book are listed in alphabetical order in the glossary.**

- **The index is also found at the back of the book. What do you see in the index?** (names, words, page numbers) **You can use the index to find a specific name or subject and know what page it is on in the book. Sometimes the subject appears on more than one page.**

Distribute a copy of "Bubbles, Bubbles, Bubbles" to each student. Read aloud the Strategy box on the student printout. Point out that the Strategy box includes words for all the text features just reviewed. Explain: **You can use the words to talk about text features and where to find information.**

Model using text features to find information: **What page number would you turn to if you wanted to read about bubbles made from soap? The table of contents helps me find topics and page numbers in the book. I will look at the table of contents. I see that Section 2 is titled Soap Bubbles. It is on page 6. I would turn to page 6 to read about the bubbles that soap makes.**

Practice and Apply: Using Text Features

Explain that the group will practice using text features to find information and answer questions.

Point to the Section 3 title. Have a volunteer read it aloud. Ask: **What does this information tell you?** (Possible response: It tells me that I would learn about liquid bubbles in Section 3, on page 10.)

Point to the heading *Making Glass Bubbles* on page 12. Ask a volunteer to read it aloud. Ask: **What is this text feature called?** (a heading) **What does the heading help you understand?** (Possible response: The heading helps me understand that this section will be about glass bubbles.) Read aloud the paragraph under the heading.

Point out the bolded word *blowpipe*. Ask: **Where would you look to find the meaning of this word?** (in the glossary) **What is the meaning of blowpipe?** (a long, metal pipe used to blow glass)

Point to the index. Ask: **On what pages would you look to find more information about blowing bubbles?** (on pages 3, 11, and 12)

Tell students they will now work in pairs to use text features to find information. Assign each pair a question using one of the following prompts. After pairs have discussed the answers to their assigned questions, have volunteers share their answers and tell where they found the information.

- **Why are blowpipes long?** (to keep the hot glass a safe distance away from the glassblower)
- **On what pages would you look to find out how to make bubbles using dish soap?** (on page 7)
- **What is the meaning of the word force?** (strength and energy)

Check Progress

Distribute the Comprehension Questions to each student. To check individual progress, have each student answer the questions in writing on the student page.

1. What is the meaning of *film*?

(a thin layer of liquid)

2. On what pages would you find more information about doing experiments with bubbles?

(on pages 9 and 11)

3. What is a hexagon?

(a shape with six sides)

4. What does the image help you understand?

(Possible responses: what a blowpipe looks like; how a glassblower holds a blowpipe)

Check individual responses. If the student can correctly answer the questions, consider the intervention successful.

Reteaching Lessons ∨

Name _____

Bubbles, Bubbles, Bubbles
Table of Contents

Strategy: Use these words to talk about text features in an informational text:

table of contents
title
heading
glossary
image
chart
caption
index

Reteaching Lessons

Glossary

blow pipe a a long, metal pipe used to blow glass

evaporates changes into a gas

film a thin layer of liquid

force strength and energy

hexagon a shape with six sides

Index

B

C

D

E

Section 4: Glass Bubbles

Making Glass Bubbles

A glassblower uses heat to melt glass. She puts the melted glass at the end of a **blowpipe**. Then she blows into the pipe very carefully and the **force** of the air causes a bubble to form.

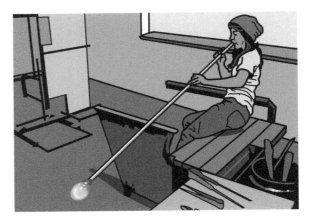

A blowpipe must be long to keep the hot glass a safe distance away from the glassblower.

12

Bubbles, Bubbles, Bubbles
Copyright © Imagine Learning, Inc.

Comprehension Questions

Use the text features in "Bubbles, Bubbles, Bubbles" to answer each question.

1. What is the meaning of *film*?

_____

2. On what pages would you find more information about doing experiments with bubbles?

_____

3. What is a hexagon?

_____

_____

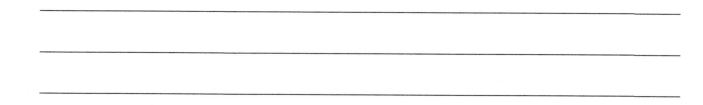

4. What does the image help you understand?

_____

_____

_____

Reteaching Lessons

LEARNING OBJECTIVE: Use informational text features to find information and understand text meaning.

LANGUAGE OBJECTIVE: Discuss informational text features using a word bank for academic language support.

Lesson Overview

Students interpret and use informational text features to find information.

Materials

- Printout of "River Otters" (one per student)
- an informational textbook to model the following text features: *table of contents, titles, headings, bold glossary words, images (photographs, charts, maps), captions, glossary, index*
- Printouts of Comprehension Questions (one per student)

Teach and Model: Using Text Features

Tell students they will use text features to find information and answer questions.

Review informational texts and text features. Say: *You already know that there are different types of texts.* Ask: *How are informational texts different from literature?* (Possible response: Informational texts have facts that tell about a topic. Literature can be a story or poetry.)

Explain: *Informational texts often have many important parts that can help us find and understand information.*

Use a familiar informational textbook to point out the important parts of a text as you review each part.

- *This is a <u>table of contents</u>. What do you notice about it?* (It's at the beginning of the book; it has page numbers; the information is in a list.) *The table of contents is a list of topics and page numbers that to help you know where to go.*
- *This is a <u>title</u>. What do you notice about it?* (It is bigger; it is at the top of the page; it has darker [bold] letters.) *The title tells you what you will be reading about.*
- *These are <u>headings</u>. What do you notice about them?* (They are bold; bigger; at the beginning of a section.) *Headings go above paragraphs of text. They give you clues about what you will learn in each section.*
- *These are <u>bold words</u>. What do you notice about them?* (The letters are darker/thicker.) *They are important words that can help you understand the topic. You can use the glossary to look up any of the bold words from the book and find their definitions.*
- *These are <u>images</u>. Images can be photos, charts, or maps. How can they help you as you read informational texts?* (They show us what things look like; show colors; give more information.) *Pictures, charts, and maps can give you more information about a topic.*
- *What do you notice underneath the charts and pictures?* (words, sentences, small text) *The words underneath are called <u>captions</u>. Captions explain what you see in the image.*
- *The <u>glossary</u> is usually found at the back of the book. What do you see in the glossary?* (words, definitions, page numbers) *All the bold words from the whole book are listed in alphabetical order in the glossary.*
- *The <u>index</u> is also found at the back of the book. What do you see in the index?* (names, words, page numbers) *You can use the index to find a specific name or subject and know what page it is on in the book. Sometimes the subject appears on more than one page.*

Practice and Apply: Using Text Features

Distribute a copy of "River Otters" to each student. Point out that the Strategy box includes a word bank with all the text features just reviewed. Explain that students will practice using text features to find information and answer questions.

 Imagine Learning®

Ask a volunteer to point to the Section 1 title on page 2. Ask another volunteer to read it aloud. Ask: **What information does this title tell us?** (Possible response: The title tells us that this part of the book is about where river otters live.)

Point to the heading *Where are the River Otters?* on page 2. Ask a volunteer to name the text feature. (a heading) Ask: **What does the heading tell us?** (Possible response: The heading tells us that this part of the text will be about where river otters can be found.) Have students choral read the paragraph under the heading.

Ask a volunteer to find a bold word in the paragraph. Ask: **What bold word did you find?** (dens) Have another volunteer find the meaning of the word *den* and read aloud the definition. Ask: **Where did you find the meaning of the word?** (in the glossary)

Tell students they will now work in pairs to use text features to find information. Read aloud the heading *Make a Home* and the paragraph. Have pairs work together to answer the following questions. After pairs have discussed each question, have volunteers share their answers.

Ask the following questions: **What does the heading tell us?** (Possible response: The heading tells us that this part of the text will be about how river otters make homes.)

Where would you look if you wanted to find out what river otters eat? (Possible responses: The table of contents shows that Section 3 "Hungry Otters" is on page 10; the index shows that pages 10 and 12 talk about food, so I can turn to those pages to find out what river otters eat.)

What does the index tell you about the word home? (Possible response: The index tells me the word *home* is found on pages 2 to 3, and page 5.)

What does the image help us understand? (Possible response: The image helps me understand what a river otter looks like.)

Check Progress

Distribute the Comprehension Questions to each student. To check individual progress, have each student answer the questions in writing.

1. What does the map show?

The map shows (where river otters live in North America.)

2. What is the title of the next section after "Homes for a River Otter"?

The next section is titled (Moving Around)

3. What is the definition of the word *carnivore*?

(an animal that eats meat)

4. On what page should you look for more information about an otter's family? (on page 5)

Check individual responses. If the student can correctly answer the questions, consider the intervention successful.

Name _____

River Otters
Table of Contents

Strategy: Use these words to talk about text features in an informational text:

table of contents	*image*
title	*map*
heading	*caption*
glossary	*index*

Glossary

burrow a passage in the ground made by an animal for a place to live

carnivore an animal that eats meat

crayfish small freshwater animals that are similar to lobsters

den the shelter of a wild animal

ecosystem all the living things in a specific area

Index

F

family, 5

food, 10, 12

form, 7

H

home, 2–3, 5

Section 1: Homes for a River Otter

Where are the River Otters?

Scientists believe that over 100,000 river otters live in North America. No matter what area they live in, they build their **dens** in water.

The colored area shows where river otters live in North America.

Make a Home

The best home for a river otter is by a river, lake, or swamp. River otters  make a **burrow** near the edge of the water with many tunnels to and from the water.

2

River Otters
Copyright © Imagine Learning, Inc.

Imagine Learning®

Comprehension Questions

Use the text features in "River Otters" to answer each question.

1. What does the map show?

The map shows _____

_____

2. What is the title of the next section after "Homes for a River Otter"?

The next section is titled _____

_____

3. What is the definition of the word *carnivore*?

_____

_____

4. On what page should you look for more information about an otter's family?

_____

_____

Comprehension Questions: River Otters

Reteaching Lessons ∨

Made in the USA
Middletown, DE
29 December 2021